I
Was
There
All
Along

A Memoir
By
Margo T Krasne

I Was There All Along – ISBN 978-0-9979654-9-0

Library of Congress Control Number: 2016962623

PUBLISHED BY:
SIMPLY GOOD PRESS
WWW.SIMPLYGOODPRESS.COM
MONTCLAIR, NJ USA

This book is dedicated with gratitude to all my families:
Those who were with me from birth
And those I created along the way.

Part I

Oh, dear, what can the matter be?

Dear, dear, what can the matter be?

Oh, dear, what can the matter be?

All of my pieces look dead!

*—There must be something you can do
to resurrect them.*

—Jews do not get resurrected.

—Not true. One did.

Fall 1986

I was turning 49. Exhausted. Depleted. About to lose my home.
Where the hell had it all gone? I was supposed to be somebody. I'd
graduated from one of the best professional acting schools in the
city—if not the country. I'd run a department at a major advertising agency. Two of my sculptures were in a museum for Christ's
sake. And there I was—curled up in a chair staring out my window contemplating a leap. If the damn panes hadn't been so heavy I
might have done it. Then again, the building next to ours came up
to our third floor and as I was on the seventh—well, it's one thing
to end it all with one grand flourish and quite another to deal with
broken bones, a smashed face, and the likelihood I'd be institution-
ally interned for an extended period of time. Not to mention I had

two cats that relied on my caretaking. One who needed subcutaneous fluids injected twice daily—by me of course.

It didn't help that I was also coping with what was termed Adult-Onset Asthma brought on most likely by stress, cigarettes (lots), toxic materials, along with a genetic predisposition to the disease (who knew?) The asthma could get so severe I'd have to race to an ER for a steroidal and oxygen fix or risk expiring. Of course, I could have let the asthma take over —asphyxiation certainly a solution to all my problems—but then there were the cats. One thing to take my life. Quite another to take theirs. Besides, it's hard not to fight for air when one is being deprived of it. Amazingly, I still had a few friends left, one in particular who phoned daily hounding me to get to a shrink.

"You need help, for God's sake!"

"It's normal to be depressed after a mother dies," I argued.

"Not this much!"

Dorothy, who by now was like an older sister, was kind enough not to say, "You'd been waiting for your mom to die for years, so what are you really crying about?" as I'd said those very words to myself often in between bouts of wracking sobs. There came a day—partially to get Dorothy off my back, partially because I was getting bored with me—I gave up and started asking around for names of therapists. Now you would think living in New York City it would be an easy task to find one, but not if you had my list of parameters.

My List:

First: No Freudians! I had no desire to go to a shrink who saw sexual implications in the nuances of daily living.

Second: He or she, preferably the latter, had to be within a reasonable distance of my home. Yes, I had hours to fill, but I saw no reason to spend them on public transportation. Besides, considering the state I was in, I didn't think I'd find mental health in just a few visits—not to mention, Mom had lived on the Upper East Side and I found it incredibly painful to be near her old neighborhood where a lot of shrinks had planted themselves.

Third: No one straight out of shrink school. My first shrink, well really my second, Dr. Bookhalter, had said a shrink had to have experienced loss to be worth her salt. (I called her Dr. Bookhalter to her face and Bookie or Dr. B when speaking about her to friends. My family referred to her as 'Across the Street,' as in "What did 'Across the Street' say about that?" Well, her office was situated diagonally across the street from my parents' apartment.) In other words, I wanted someone who'd dealt with death, though how I expected to find that out eludes me.

And last: No guru-types with cult followings. The kind whose patients knew each other, slept together, slept with the doctor, all that crazy seventies stuff. Not as if I'd ever been to one of those, but I certainly had read they were out there—often with homes in the Hamptons.

Oh, and one more thing. It would be great if she (or he) were straight. Better yet, married with children as my relationships with men, or recent lack thereof, were sorely in need of help to say the least. (Turned out Dr. B had been gay—not that I'd noticed at the time. To me she just looked like Margaret Rutherford, the old English actress who wore tweeds and sensible, laced-up shoes. I don't think it had made a difference one way or another. But then, you never know, do you?)

I don't recall who gave me the first shrink's name, but he couldn't see me and sent me on to someone else as did most of the others often giving me more than one to call. I started to write each name on its own 3" x 5" index card and place it on my counter. After a month the counter —all 6' x 3' of it—was full. Besides their names and who had recommended them, I made notes of what was wrong with each. One was too expensive; another too far away, another could see me, but only now and then as she was overbooked, and on it went. Some cards had nothing but a name and number written on them because my call was never returned. However, one doctor did call back, at 11 o'clock on a Friday night no less! He gave me a minute or two to explain my situation then burst into a full-blown reprimand, his voice seething with fury.

"If you really wanted help, you'd have found it by now."

I'd never heard a shrink so angry. This being late on a Friday night, I decided his tirade emanated from hours upon hours of having to listen to his patients' plaints and not being able to tell them to "grow up!" He was wrong about me, of course. I just didn't want to make another mistake—I mean 4 years with Bookie some twenty years earlier and look where I was. He did, however, give me a name along with a directive: "Get off your ass and go!"

If only to prove him wrong, I made an appointment. At least this shrink was on 4th and Broadway, within walking distance of my loft. Did I mention I lived on 20th Street between Fifth Avenue and Broadway in what's called the Flatiron District? Anyway, the first thing that hit me as I entered the waiting room was the Muzak in the background. Now I can't abide Muzak at any time, but in a shrink's office? When she came out to get me, I couldn't resist.

"There's Muzak playing!" I said.

"Does it bother you?"

"Doesn't it bother you?" my tone more than implying that if it didn't, it damn well should.

She explained she shared the space and the lease holder wanted

Muzak, which translated to me she was not experienced enough to have her own office where she could call the shots. She certainly dressed straight out of school. But then, who was I to talk? I hadn't even been able to figure out what to wear to my own mother's funeral.

"How can I help?" she asked.

And before I could say a word, my tears started flowing. I blubbered through explaining my mother had died five months before and that I'd been a sculptor who no longer sculpts. Then, keeping my eyes trained on her to catch her reaction, I warily offered up my litmus test: That for all the years I'd sculpted, I'd never felt like an artist. And what does she say?

"But you sold your work, yes?"

Dear God! I mean what the hell does selling one's work have to do with believing you're an artist? Her question sent me into even more despair. Even so, without any other place to turn, I made a second appointment. At least I could cry in her office without fear of reprimand.

Two days later Pablo, my cat of sixteen years, died. He'd been on his way out for the last two, but was considerate enough to stay around long enough for me to bury Mom. I was relieved and heartbroken all at once. He'd washed my hair every night of his life, attacked anyone who tried to come into the bedroom if I was in it, peed in the shoes of those men who managed to get by him and basically was the steadiest love of my life. Mischa was left, but he, partly of my doing, was more aloof. Who could blame him? I had doted on Pablo.

I didn't tell the shrink that I was still looking around for someone else, but when a financial advisor, whom I'd consulted to handle the monies Mom left me, gave me the name of hers ("My husband and I both go to her. And oh, she's gay, but none of us care...") straight or gay, I made the call. Perhaps she would get it.The only time this one had was ten days off at 10:45 in the morning. I took it. Then Regina, a painter friend, called and reminded me she knew someone who ran a woman's referral service—had even mentioned her to me at another one of my low points, but I'd rejected the idea out of hand. Her friend was a German. To this day I can't believe how thoughtless I'd been since Regina was also German—albeit married to a Jew. In my defense, I hadn't been able to imagine spilling my guts to someone about whose heritage I was more than a little conflicted. But as it was only for a referral, here again, I made the call. (I'd heard one should always get three bids, of course this referred to contractors, not shrinks.)

Regina's shrink offered me an appointment on the same day as the financial gal's. When I mentioned I was seeing someone else before her and the idea of reciting the whole damn saga twice in a day would wipe me out, in a voice, barely above a whisper, as if telephones were something to be wary of, she told me I'd have hours in between to recoup. At least that's what I think she said. Between the wisps of an accent, and the whisper, it was hard to tell.

Both shrinks' offices were within walking distance of the loft—a few blocks from each other in the West Village. The gay shrink's office was a drab room, painted a cold cheap white, the kind that comes in ten gallon cans from hardware stores. The only furniture: two black ladder-back chairs—one for the shrink, the other for the patient. A black and white photograph of a cityscape hung on the wall behind her, framing her head. She was overweight and butch. I knew immediately the weight, more than the fact she was gay, would be an issue for me. I didn't tell her that, just said I wasn't sure how comfortable I'd be with her being gay. She asked whether it was because my family treated homosexuality as a disease, or a sign of insanity. I said probably both. Which was true. When I was in my junior year in high school, my brother decided I could be a lesbian and brought his concerns to my parents. His reasoning? The music teacher at the school had taken me to see Amahl and The Night Visitors. That she had time on her hands because she was dating a married man—something I couldn't tell anyone, even in self-defense, or she'd be fired—along with the fact I was one of the only students eager for her attention—was all beside the point. My brother was a master of deflection. If Dad was getting on his case, my brother would rally the family to focus on me. I left this shrink with a thank you and a polite, "I'm seeing a few other doctors before I make up my mind." We both knew I wouldn't be coming back.

I arrived at the Perry Street brownstone early. I didn't know whether to ring the bell or sit on the stoop. I decided to ring as it was too cold to remain outside. The buzzer went off and in I went. The hallway was dark. There was a stairway leading to the second floor and a bench with a few magazines outside a door. I figured this had to be it. I sat in the darkened hall and waited. To the minute of my appointed time, the door opened, a man quickly exited— I could only see his back—and a woman beckoned me in. Memory has it she was in a colorful red and orange print with beads around her neck and long dangling red earrings. But as this was November, the image had to come from another time. My guess is I didn't pay much attention to her. How could I? The room before me was unlike anything I'd ever seen.

This was not an antiseptic, impersonal, blank slate on which patients could project their fantasies. Here every bit of space was filled with what had to be mementos from a life lived to its fullest. The white walls, what you could see of them, served as a huge mat for the numerous framed photographs of Bushmen, lions, zebras, rainforests, rustic abodes and archeological digs she had obviously visited. There were unframed paintings whose caliber ranged from God awful to extraordinarily expert. I could only assume they were acquired for emotional rather than aesthetic reasons. (The one of Freud with a cigar staring down at a couch with a nude reclining

Maja, certainly wasn't reverential.) There were African dolls, phallic symbols, animal bones, colored glass objects, *chotzkes* my father would have called them, crammed onto the mantle of the fireplace and the two window sills. An Eames chair and ottoman were on one side of the room and opposite a daybed made up to look like a sofa where she motioned me to sit. Even this was loaded with various sized stuffed animals of unidentifiable lineage; the rugs, fabrics on the chairs and pillows were blends of red, orange and purples.

Then there were the books. Thousands of them crammed onto the bookcases—more like slats of wood haphazardly nailed together set upon cinder blocks looking as if they'd collapse at any moment from the weight piled on. The shelving went from floor to ceiling, filled two entire walls, then extended into a hallway. With no shiny new book covers in the stacks, clearly there wasn't a best seller in the lot—all tomes of erudition that had been read and reread.

As for the shrink, she was blonde, (did I mention that was the color my mother had kept her hair?) thin, almost wiry with chiseled features. After ushering me in, she plopped herself down on the Eames chair simultaneously tossing her feet onto the ottoman, and draped her hand over its arm. I wouldn't notice the mop of a living, breathing dog stretched out next to her chair for some time. She smiled—a small taut smile—and waited as did I. Then she asked why I was there. I admit to being more than a bit taken aback. I thought I'd made myself quite clear when I made the appointment. "I need a referral," I said.

"I need to know a bit more about you," she responded and nodded for me to start.

For the second time that day I went through my litany of despair: "My cat just died. My mother died—not in that order. I'm without a career. Sorry, I can't stop crying." And then, again, my eyes trained on her, my litmus test: "All the years I sculpted, I never felt like an artist."

And she nodded. I could feel my muscles begin to relax. Clearly she got it. Here was someone who did not think of artists as special, who understood them—even those who didn't believe they were one.

"Do you still sculpt? Regina tells me you are very good."

"God, no! Finished. Done. Finito! Can you imagine there are those who still introduce me as a sculptor? I mean if you're not doing, then you're not, now are you? It's been over two years since I've had my hands in clay." Whatever pleasure derived from the compliment, I brushed aside. What was past was past.

Her high energy stood in sharp contrast to my own to-the-bone lethargy. I tried to sit erect, but my muscles kept collapsing in on themselves. Nothing appeared to exist inside me. Well, there wasn't, was there? I mean a lack of a self, a perfectly centered inner being—something I had been seeking most of my life, was why I was asking for help in the first place. It was what Martha Graham—the great avant-garde choreographer and modern dancer—called a core. I remember her standing in front of our class, pulled up so much taller than her actual height, her hand swooping down below her pubic area, her fingers shooting upwards seeming to reach through the ceiling towards the sky. "It should be a rod of steel," she'd cry, or something close to that. How I yearned to possess that rod. To develop an inner strength that wouldn't sway with whatever winds washed over me. If I were religious, I could call my search a quest for the Holy Grail of Being. But as I was not religious, and a Jew, it wouldn't work. I sunk amidst the stuffed animals wondering where I'd get the strength to recite the rest of the saga.

"And when did your Mom die?" she asked.

"June. June 3rd to be exact."

"And your Dad? Is he still alive?"

"No. Died in '75. Listen, shouldn't I have stopped crying by now?"

And very slowly, as if to make certain each word penetrated my psyche, she answered, "The loss of what might have been is always greater than the loss of what was." Then she pushed the obligatory box of tissues towards me.

Of course there was no way I could take one. If I wasn't going to be seeing her on a regular basis, I didn't feel right using her tissues. As my mom often said, I understood pennies far more than dollars. How could I not? She had trained me to look at the right side of every menu before even considering anything on the left—something I still do even if someone else is paying. Forget what food I might crave. And as for my father, he would serve up a large bowl of Beluga caviar with all the fixings while running around turning out lights. I reached into my bag for my own tissues just as she lit up a cigarette.

"I have asthma!" I cried out expecting her to put it out. But all she did was open the window behind her. "Got asthma two years ago. Smoked four packs a day for twenty years. Quit cold turkey." Obviously, if she had a brain in her head, she'd do the same.

"Good for you," was all I got back. I decided if it was only going to be one session, I could put up with her smoking and reached for my inhaler, in case. Then she asked what I did all day.

Now that surprised me. I thought she could tell from my wardrobe: a dull brown tweed jacket, brown pants and flat shoes, the same outfit my neighbor Anna, a published author, wore. "I'm writing," I answered and told her how two years ago I'd found myself unable to walk into the studio part of the loft—which for all intents and purposes was the largest area. Described how I had started pushing things back, re-draping the plastic that had hung across to protect my drawings from the clay and metal dust, so that it would protect me from everything having to do with my art.

"Now I only walk in there to change the kitty litter."

She remained silent. The interest on her face signaling me to continue.

"I started reading Lessing's The Golden Notebook. Kept waiting to see if her narrator went back to writing as if that would tell me whether I'd sculpt again. But I knew I wouldn't. Physically couldn't. Too many disappointments. Too many rejections."

"And the writing? How did that start?"

"Now I know this is going to sound weird but one morning, February 24th to be exact—I marked it on my calendar, isn't that crazy?—anyway, that morning I was sitting at my counter having coffee and I looked over at the typewriter on my dining room table and out comes, 'Well, Phillip Roth, you sure have nothing on me!' I practically jumped out of my skin. I had never talked out loud to myself before. But it definitely was me speaking. Well, within minutes I had paper in the Olivetti and I've been writing ever since. I don't want you to think I'm comparing myself to Roth. Don't even like a lot of what he writes. I was simply identifying with his *kvetching.* That's Yiddish for complaining."

"I know from *kvetching.*" For a German she sounded a lot like a Jew. "And what did you *kvetch* about?"

"A sculptor who couldn't sculpt. Nothing too autobiographical. Put a lot of it in nursery rhyme form."

I also told her I'd taken a few writing classes and that I'd made friends with a writer. What I couldn't tell her was that I had no desire for another career in the Arts. That the only reason I was writing was if I stopped, I had no idea as to who or what the hell I would be.

It began to dawn on me I shouldn't look any further. She was the third of the shrinks and certainly seemed the best of the lot. Besides, I was tired. Had no desire to repeat my history one more time. To hell with the fact she was German—I'd certainly slept with enough of them—and as long as she was willing to open a window when she smoked, then hey, why not? Clearly she had a life. Possible she could show me how to get one as well.

"I've decided. I'm coming to you," I announced towards the end of our next session. And did she say, good or great? No! Just,

"We'll see."

Then she opened a large black appointment book, the kind with hours slotted in fifteen minute intervals, and began to search through page after calendar page for an available time. This would have been perfectly normal were it not for the fact there was not one word of writing on any of them. Yet there she was, pen poised, poring over each empty time slot until finally, she stopped, looked up and said, "How about next Monday at 5:45?"

"There's nothing on the page."

"I only write down a change or a new patient appointment."

"How many patients do you have?"

"Twenty-seven. Plus I run two groups."

I was in awe. It took an incredible intellect to pull that off. Then the buzzer rang. I glanced at the clock—she had two: one faced her; one the patient, i.e. me. It was 6:30 to the minute. She pressed the intercom behind her, rose and proceeded to show me to the door. I took my time getting there.

I couldn't get her, or the room, out of my mind. We'd had a "red room" when I was growing up. Unlike hers, ours was designed by a decorator. It had deep red wall-to-wall carpeting, matching red walls and ceiling. The furniture was also red except for two large white leather arm chairs. It was like being swathed in red bunting—a den in the true sense of the word. It was where my father came home to—my mother having made certain there was ice and water on the bar ready for his scotch, and hors d'ouevres on the card table. I'd loved that room. Definitely! Her office was where I belonged.

I brought slides of my sculptures to the next session. I needed her to understand that no matter how I felt about not being an artist, it had nothing to do with the quality of my work. I held my breath as she looked at them waiting for her reaction.

"They're very good," she said.

"You sound just like de Kooning."

"Oh?"

"That's what he said."

"Really? When?"

"Probably about four or five years ago. I was visiting a friend out on the Island and one day he told me to grab my slides and come with him. I used to carry them everywhere in case I met a potential buyer. My friend wouldn't say where we were going and I almost passed out when we pulled up in front of de Kooning's house. He'd been one of my gods. My friend, who didn't know de Kooning, dragged me up the driveway. I behaved like a dog on a leash on the way to the vet. He knocked, de Kooning answered, and once my friend explained how much I adored his work, the master let us in. I was overwhelmed with emotion. Thankfully, de Kooning had cats and I immediately went down on the floor to play with them. There were drawings lying all over the floor. Can you imagine? I actually sat amongst his drawings? Then my friend says, 'Hey, Margo, don't you want to show Mr. de Kooning your slides?' I still couldn't speak, tears of awe rolling down my cheeks. All I could do was hold up the packet of slides which my friend then passed to de Kooning. I felt ill. He put on his glasses, sat down, and studied each page. Then he says, in a voice filled with surprise. 'My, they're really good!' I'm sure he'd thought I was a total lunatic."

"But, unlike de Kooning, I didn't sound surprised, did I?" she asked.

"No," I admitted.

"You don't need to validate your work, Margo. I can see for myself that it's quite good."

That really did it—proved she could see right through me.

"I want to clean house," I told her as I took out my new set of 3 x 5 index cards on which I had written what I wanted to discuss. "From top to bottom." I figured if I acted like a permanent patient, she'd treat me as one. "Attic to basement: art, careers, family, the works," I told her. At least before I died, I should understand what went wrong. Why, for example, I probably held the record for not being able to sustain a relationship with the opposite sex for more than a few intense weeks—unless the man lived miles away. Still, as I hadn't been to bed with anyone in over two years, I decided to leave the man thing alone—there were many more pressing problems. "So can I come to you? Obviously I don't need a referral."

She gave a slight nod.

"Does that mean I can?"

"Let's see how it goes."

"Why can't you just say yes?"

At the end of the session she headed to the door, opened it and waited for me to leave.

"What should I call you?" I asked.

"Susanne, is fine." She pronounced it Suz-anna.

At the next session, I asked what she charged.

"Eighty-five. And I don't take insurance. Nor will I put in for it."

I was more than a bit surprised, not about the insurance. Just that Dr. B had charged a hundred twenty-five some twenty years earlier. My dad believed you got what you paid for so he'd only pay top dollar or do without. I brushed aside the thought that maybe she wasn't as good as I imagined. Well, if nothing else, I could afford her.

I could tell by the slight smile that crossed her face when I brought out my cards that Susanne found them a source of amusement. But I wanted to be sure she had whatever she needed to know as quickly as possible so that we could get down to the real stuff—though what that was, I had no idea.

"Quick recap," I began. "I was the baby of the family. My sister, Bebe—her actual name Bernice though she preferred Mike- anyway, she was fifteen years older, my brother Chuck twelve. She's dead."

"How and when did your sister die?"

"Cancer. Breast. Got it at thirty-seven; died five years later. She had a Down Syndrome baby—they called them Mongoloids then …"

"I know what they were called, Margo."

"Right! Anyway, she was born the year before the first cancer operation." I talked as quickly as I possibly could, not wanting to waste a minute.

"Did your sister have other children?"

I found this line of questioning unnecessary and totally beside the point. But, I answered. "A boy and a girl. Girl first, boy nine years later, then the Down Syndrome baby, then the cancer, then gone."

"How old were you?"

"Twenty-seven."

"And your brother?"

"He was turning 40."

"I meant tell me about him. Married? Children?"

"Two boys. Married when I was thirteen. To an Egyptian Jewish princess. Not that she was an actual princess, just behaved like one. And she was gorgeous. She and her twin. They spoke French. Wouldn't speak it to me. Wore flowers in their hair, can you imagine? Probably why I had my nose fixed, No that's not true. Listen, none of this is important." According to the clock, I had about a minute left. "So, I'm definitely coming to you, right?"

She appeared to nod in the affirmative, though it was hard to tell.

"Then should we discuss the German/Jewish issue?"

"It will take care of itself."

I hoped so and as soon as I got outside, I jotted it down on a new card to be brought up at a future time.

Susanne opened the next session with, "Tell me about your nose."

I couldn't believe it. A whole week had passed. "Do you take notes?"

"No."

"And you remembered a throwaway line?"

She ignored my question. "How old were you?"

"Thirteen. How do you keep it all in your head? I mean that's incredible."

"It's my job," she said brushing my awe aside.

"Yeah, but other shrinks write things down. You've got 27 patients. With me it's 28. That's a lot of crap to remember."

"Margo, nothing is crap so please don't change the subject. Tell me about having your nose fixed. Thirteen is very young to have it done."

"I'm not changing the subject. I'm commenting on what an incredible memory you have."

"Thank you, now whose idea was it?"

"Mine! Well, sort of. My dad always said I had great eyes and would be beautiful if not for the nose. Listen it was a big hook. Also, I had two teeth, close together on my hard palette, growing up toward my nose. God knows where they came from. Of course, they should have been removed, but no, the orthodontist thought he could turn them around and pull them over—how else would he send his kids to college? So he put rubber bands on them, braces on every tooth tightening them every damn Friday. I was in pain most of the time, felt like a freak. Well, I was one, wasn't I?"

"That had to be very difficult."

"Not as difficult as being tied down to a table while my darling Uncle Murray, well, he wasn't really my uncle, that's just what I called him—all my parents' friends were called Aunt or Uncle— anyway he tied me down so he could fix my chin. I hadn't even known it needed fixing." I watched her face for a reaction. Something I instinctually did when telling the story. She appeared taken aback.

"He tied you down?"

It all tumbled out. How I'd thought having my nose fixed would change my life. How I'd almost jumped on the table I'd wanted it so bad. "And just when I thought we were finished, dear Uncle Murray reached for another needle and aimed it back at me. I screamed for him to stop. Asked him what he was doing. Tried to push him away. No luck. He and his nurse tied me down. 'Just putting in a bit of cartilage. You want to be pretty, don't you?' he said. Now I knew my father had lied. I was truly ugly."

"What did your parents say?"

"For a long time I didn't remember them saying anything. I'd begged them not to pay him, but they rewarded him with two suits from Sulka's. For years I never told anyone. Not even Dr. Bookhalter the whole time I was with her. Then, a few years ago, I started feeling something growing in my chin. I thought it was the cartilage having come loose, or worse, that it had turned cancerous. I made an appointment with my dentist. His hygienist saw me first. I tried to tell her why I was there, but kept choking up. She was incredible. It took 45 minutes until I managed to get the words out and she never rushed me or tried to leave the room. Simply took an X-ray. Turned out it was only a pimple. I began to test the waters expecting anyone I told to see me in a whole new light— that of a fraud."

"Is that what you expected me to see?"

I shrugged. "Maybe. It wasn't until a friend's husband asked if the doctor was still alive and I said, 'No, why?' and he said with incredible anger, 'If he was, I'd take a gun and shoot him,' did I start to feel sort of okay. But you know the real kicker?" I waited for Susanne to say something, but she just nodded for me to continue. "Well, I decided to call Mom and go at it. 'If Murray Berger was still alive,' I said. 'I'd shoot him!' And without missing a beat— we're talking a good thirty years later—she says exactly what she said then, 'I know. You just don't have to tell anyone.' Then she added, 'Besides, we meant well.' Can you imagine? They knew all along—had been in on it from the start."

"Do you understand that her telling you not to tell anyone is what caused the shame you've felt all these years? The reason it was something to be hidden?"

"Yeah, figured that out. If it weren't for the pimple, I'd still be keeping it a secret. Guess it was time for the puss to burst."

"You were violated, Margo."

"I know."

She left it alone, but her look of condolence was enough.

———————————

At the time I began seeing Susanne, I was living with a Damocles Sword of eviction over my head. Our building had been sold and the new owners were readying our lofts for the inspectors, removing whatever walls I'd constructed, running pipes for water and waste through my ceiling to the floor below, leaving them exposed. They expected me to be gone as soon as the Certificate of Occupancy was obtained for a buyout of $100,000, unless I could flip it and get a better price.

I had no idea of where I'd go or what I'd do—having no obvious way to support myself. I hadn't had a steady job for over twenty years. To supplement whatever meagre income I derived from my sculptures and drawings, I had painted apartments, worked as a hostess at a restaurant and been an extra in commercials having gotten my union cards during my acting days and never letting them lapse. (Being an extra could entail sitting in a bikini on a beach in mid-December or standing out in the rain all night while a director tried to get the perfect shot for a 30 second commercial.) As for furniture, all I had was a bed, a sofa and matching chair my mom had helped me purchase, her old love seat, along with the

Empire breakfront that had stood in my parents' apartments from the time I was born. Of course, the breakfront looked ridiculous in the loft, but I wasn't ready to let go of one of the last vestiges of my childhood. I'd sat beneath it with my spindly knees pulled towards me, watching my father and his brothers pitch pennies in our foyer. Those were memories I couldn't part with—at least not yet.

———————————

At the end of my ninth session, two days before Christmas, Susanne pulled out her blank calendar, skipped a few pages and put a dot on a page. She'd found me a permanent slot!

"I'll see you on the 6th at 2:15."

"That's two weeks away!" I cried.

"I told you when you first started, I always take Christmas through New Year's off. As well as two weeks in February."

Obviously I hadn't paid attention. She said something else, but by then I was too upset to hear her. I pleaded with her to change her mind. "Dr. Bookhalter decided it was too precarious to leave patients over the holidays. Besides, it's also my birthday." I sounded like a spoiled child, but the idea of her leaving even for a week meant my life would be put on hold or worse.

"I am not Dr. Bookhalter and I promise you, you'll survive. When's your birthday?"

"December 30th a lousy day for a birthday. No one wants to celebrate. Everyone's resting up for the next night."

"Well, I hope you do something nice. What are you planning?"

"Some friends might come over." I left out that I'd invited at least thirty and they were going to bring the food while I'd supply the wine and incidentals. She was leaving me so she didn't need the details.

"Good. Enjoy it! And have a happy holiday."

I left feeling desolate. The next day I came down with a flu so severe the resulting asthma sent me to the ER. It looked like there was no way I could pull off the party on my actual birth date, so I grudgingly rescheduled and moved it to the 6th. I had no conscious awareness of how the date coincided with Susanne's return. Birthdays were important to me—out of proportionately so. But then growing up I'd been gypped out of more than a few. I don't remember ever having a party and the first birthday I do remember was my tenth. On that Christmas Eve, I was in my room getting ready for bed with Tessie, our all-around maid, seamstress, laundress, waitress and my adored caretaker, when my mother appeared in the doorway and announced they were off to the Waldorf for a few days. At least until the predicted blizzard passed.

"Me too?" I asked, thinking I needed a suitcase.

"No dear, just your father and I. We're concerned our windows could blow in."

I couldn't figure out why theirs' could and mine wouldn't. Both our windows faced the park. As if reading my mind, Mom added, "Ours are corner windows, dear. Yours will be fine." Then she said she'd give me her heater so both Tessie and I would have one. I didn't know enough to wonder what would happen if the electricity went out.

"Doesn't Tessie need to go home to her husband?" I asked. "I mean if there's going to be a storm."

"We've already discussed this with Tessie. She'll be fine."

But I knew Tessie better than anyone and she was anything but fine; seated on the edge of one of the beds, I watched her chapped hands play with each other as if one could calm the other down. I made one more stab. "You could sleep in the back room, couldn't you?"

"Too hard moving the beds. Easier to go to a hotel." Then Mom told me my birthday gifts were on the dining room table. "Just in case we don't get back in time." She made me promise not to open them. "Promise?" She left out that the next day was her own birthday and a great reason to get away alone with her husband. Not that I would have understood.

The blizzard of 1947 killed seventy-seven people. It went down as one of the worst blizzards the city had seen. Yet I remember nothing of the storm itself. I do not know if I slept or lay awake waiting for the windows to crack. Knowing me, probably both. The next morning Tessie and I guiltily snuck into the dining room. The entire table was filled with gifts just as Mom had said. One by one, we carefully opened the corners of each package to see if we could tell what was inside. There was everything I'd wanted: an easel, canvases, an entire set of oil paints, brushes, and turpentine. Any excitement at seeing all the presents in front of me was neutralized by extreme loneliness; whatever pleasure I could have derived depleted by my parents' absence and my guilt for not sticking to a promise. They were back in time for my birthday and I made certain to feign surprise. Still it all felt empty. No friends. Not even my brother and sister—just my mom, my dad already having left for work, and a lot of gifts on a dining room table.

My thirteenth was no better. I came down with a fever that kept me in bed. My mom kept poking her head in to see if I was okay, but it was clear she had forgotten what day it was. I didn't say anything until late in the morning but by that time I was so upset, there was no way to extract any pleasure from her, "Oh dear. I'm so sorry. Completely slipped my mind."

But the sixteenth topped them all. It was spent moving from the only home I'd known, 275 Central Park West, where I had spent hours curled up on my window sill looking out at the park with its incredible array of trees—one white dogwood in particular that annually popped its buds a month too early—to an apartment I hated. 275 was not considered one of the signature elite that dotted the avenue. That demarcation went to titled edifices such as The Majestic, The Beresford, The Eldorado, The San Remo and The Century—we had family or friends in each—but it did sport ten rooms if you included the enormous foyer and pantry—both large enough by any standard to be considered rooms in themselves. The new apartment was dark, faced another building, and the red room that had served as Dad's den was now my bedroom to be used by my parents whenever they had company. All this apartment had going for it was a Fifth Avenue address although the entrance was on a side street.

Winter 1987

January 6th came and I moved furniture, set out plates, and made a crudité. At 1:45 it was as if a fog had lifted. I suddenly remembered that I had an appointment with Susanne. I raced to her building, but once there, I behaved no differently than when I was a child and my parents returned from one of their many trips. I'd run to the door eager for their arrival, and then turn ice cold as soon as they entered. I didn't have to tell Susanne how I felt. My emotional distance made it more than clear.

"I totally forgot I had this appointment," I said still feeling strangely dislocated.

"Easier to pretend I didn't exist then to feel the pain of loss."

"I don't understand."

"Your parents left you alone a lot, correct?"

"Not alone."

"Don't be dense, Margo. Who stayed with you?" She was back at work. I was not ready to forgive her desertion.

I debated whether or not to tell her that I used to stand in the doorway of my room and scream for Anna, the cook, to see if she could hear me. She never did. But all I said was, "Governesses. Nursemaids. Whoever."

"In other words, you were left alone."

The irony did not escape me. For years I'd complained about my parents to anyone who would listen and now that they were no longer here, I was defending them to the hilt. I remained quiet. Finally, the silence too obvious, I changed subjects and mentioned that on the way over I'd passed a number of young mothers carrying their child in a harness. "Haven't seen these before," I said.

Susanne asked if I'd ever wanted children and I told her no and gave her my standard answer. "Only wanted to be pregnant for a day somewhere in the eighth month to see what it was like. Had you?" I added, not expecting an answer. "Wanted children?"

And she said, yes, yes she had.

"Then why didn't you?"

"Couldn't. Cancer. Hysterectomy."

I didn't know what to say. Dr. B never told me personal stuff. I was surprised, but even more so when she said she'd like me to try something. "I want you to pretend you have a child until I see you again."

"What do you mean, 'have a child?'"

"Just what I said. I want for you to pretend you have a child to take care of. So, how will you take it home?"

I couldn't believe what I was hearing. A chill of doubt ran through me. Was she one of those new wave therapists? Exactly whom I swore I wouldn't go to? I managed to tell her that was crazy. That I didn't believe in role plays. We went back and forth for what seemed endless: —I can't. —You can. —Don't make me.

—I'm not making you. —Please, this is nuts! Now I was really scared. Bad enough I'd bought her book on sadomasochism and read her bio which stated she was a founding member of the Gay Alliance—I had pushed aside the thought she might be gay because Regina had told me she'd been married. But a fake child? This was too much.

"I have guests coming. There's no way I can take care of a child—pretend or not," I told her thinking that would end it.

But no, she came back with, "You could always hire a sitter."

And I took the bait. "No way! I was brought up with nursemaids. I'm not giving my kid a sitter."

She just smiled. "I repeat. How will you take your child home?"

I told her I wouldn't push an imaginary carriage through the streets. "For God's sake. They'll haul me away."

She sat and waited for me to fill the silence.

I caved. "All right, I'll use a harness."

Surprisingly, I found the walk home comforting as I imagined an infant close to my breast—like a pillow one curls up with when feeling abandoned. Once home, I placed the baby on the bed, told the imaginary sitter to keep an eye on it, went about preparing for the party and obsessing as to whether or not my brother would show up having refused to give me an rsvp answer all week long.

My brother Chuck had never been a constant physical presence in my life. He'd been off to college when I was four, to war when I was five, and back to college when I was seven. However, when he did make an appearance, the apartment's usual silence would be replaced by a whirlwind of noise and laughter. I lived for his visits—much like Brenda Starr of the funnies who had waited for her lover although with Chuck there was no black orchid to announce his arrival. Chuck's visits were brief; the excitement fleeting—the anticipation leading up to them exquisite. When he was home he played music on the phonograph—his extensive collection of 78's consisting of Benny Goodman, Xavier Cugat, The Andrew Sisters and Tommy Dorsey. He taught me to dance, placing my feet on his shoes and showing me how to move my hips. At other times, he would pretend to be an ape—his normally handsome face contorted, arms over head, all six feet of him lumbering after Mom and me, scaring both of us. I hated when he did that, but it never stopped him; it also never stopped my relishing his attention. I was a puppet on a string where he was concerned—his moods, decisions, actions often provoked in me an intense emotional response. I could be filled with joy one minute, anger the next; reduced to tears or convulsed in laughter. He'd been given permission to name me when I was born and did so after the character Margo Lane of The Shadow—a 1937 radio show starring Orson Welles and Agnes Moorhead. (As a toddler I created an imaginary friend I named Mrs. Lane. Mom sat on her one day killing her off. Clearly I knew early on my best friend was me. I also knew when and how to dispense with her.)

And so here I was, these many years later, making his arrival at my birthday the center of my attention. At about eight o'clock he showed up along with his wife. Within seconds I went from the emotional high of a teenage girl upon seeing the object of her latest crush walk in the door, to a mixture of rage and fear. He'd only come to say good-bye in case he died—he was going in for triple by-pass surgery the next day. After he left it dawned on me I hadn't checked on the baby for hours. I raced in to where I had placed her on the bed, only to find all the guests' coats piled high. It was one helluva party. My brother could die and I had killed off my kid.

Susanne's take on the evening was simply, "Your reaction to the child was your mother's reaction to you."

"I didn't need an exercise, Susanne, to know how they treated me. Besides, Mom wasn't the primary caregiver—my governesses were—and you said that was who the child responded to!"

"Governess or no governess, your mother was the primary care-giver and it's in the mother's eyes that a child sees whether or not it's wanted."

I couldn't wait for the session to end.

Chuck didn't die. As a matter of fact, only a few days later he was home peddling away on his stationary bike to a set of big band tapes I had put together for him and calling to boast how great he felt. Once again my heart soared: two days later it sank. He had contracted a staph infection and was back in the hospital tethered to intravenous lines filled with antibiotics and steroids. A man who raged after two martinis now became a volcano spewing anger at every turn. He refused to see me. Only our brother-in-law, Buddy, his wife Marcia (the woman Bud married after my sister died) and one of Chuck's closest friends, a shrink, were allowed in.

"Why do you insist on going?" Susanne asked.

"What will they think of me if I don't?"

"Who's they?"

"My cousin for one. He calls every day to see how Chuck is. How can I tell him I don't know?"

"Tell him the truth. That your brother is behaving irrationally and you've been told to stay away."

I couldn't. I went almost daily, only to be turned back each time. I don't remember ever feeling as alone, discarded and shamed. A sad, gaunt, spinster shrouded in black.

"It's how I feel I look," I told Susanne. "What everyone sees."

She just repeated for me to stay away.

As ready as I was to pour out my soul to Susanne for mending, I held some things close. How do you tell a shrink, who you're sure is assessing whether or not you're sane, that you're convinced your dead parents are listening in on your conversations? That whenever you say something bad about your father you can see him circling overhead in his navy Sulka bathrobe, getting ready to sweep down upon you like a vulture ready to pluck out your eyes? Mom was up there as well, though only to calm him down. It wasn't total madness on my part. After she died and I returned to the loft, I could feel her presence. Sometimes when I was looking for something and couldn't find it, in frustration I'd let out a, "Mom, help!" and in seconds my hand would be on it. It happened to me at home, in a store, even once when I emerged from a subway disoriented not knowing where exactly I was. I whispered, "Christ Mom, where the hell am I?" and voila! My eyes lit on a street sign that told me in which direction to go. Now I know one could chalk this up to coincidence, which is exactly what Susanne did, when I finally opened up.

"That's magical thinking! You and your mother were on the phone daily. You were used to being in touch with her. She's gone, Margo."

"I know when she left, Susanne. I was standing in my closet, and just like that I knew she was gone. Well, the very next call I got was the one telling me Chuck was back in the hospital. I had no doubt she went to be with him."

"Coincidence! And they're not listening in."

"Wish I could believe you."

"Did your parents eavesdrop?" she asked.

I could only nod. Then in a low voice I told her how Mom listened in on my phone calls. "I know she wanted to know if I was bitching about her—which half the time I was."

"And your Dad?"

If I was paying good money to get help, I knew I had to risk his wrath and tell Susanne all, so in a small voice I recounted how my father craved perfection in his women, intruding into our lives. He monitored Mom's and my bowel movements. He shaved Mom's underarms and wanted to shave mine. I refused; he sulked. He lectured my sister and her husband as to what they should wear to bed. He, pajamas instead of underwear; she, a sexy negligee rather than her husband's pajama top. (How this even became a topic of conversation beats me.) He begged my sister to keep her legs raised whenever and wherever possible—her calves not slim enough for his taste. It was the only part of her anatomy with which he found fault. Forget that when she was eighteen the producer, Michael Todd, had spotted her at the races and asked my father if he could cast her as a showgirl in one of his productions. (The reason my brother-in-law had nicknamed her Mike.) Or, that she was married to a man who found her more than sexy. "Put those legs up!" was Dad's admonition whenever in her presence. "And he'd stand outside my bathroom demanding I stay in the tub a full twenty minutes. I'd pull myself out of the water so slowly that even with his ear pressed to the door, he couldn't hear me. Then I'd sit on the toilet with a towel wrapped around me until the twenty minutes were up."

Susanne remained silent, waiting to see if there was more.

There was, but just in case Dad could actually hear me, I rose to his defense. "He never slapped me, Susanne. Just once, after I'd done something to upset Mom. I was so shocked, I slapped him back."

More silence.

I filled it. "We were in my sister's hospital room. Chuck's wife and I on either side of her bed trying to make her comfortable. Susanne, she was bloated, disfigured, it was awful. Anyway, Dad walked in and suddenly her eyes opened and she sees him at the end of the bed and out comes, 'See Dad, my legs are up!' And he was pleased! My sister-in-law and I left the room wanting to throw up. Not Dad. He was proud as a peacock. Headed to the waiting room to tell everyone what she'd said."

I decided to bring a nursery rhyme I'd written to our next session. I even read it aloud.

"Baa Baa Black Sheep, You're stubborn as ten mules.

—Oh Sir, dear Sir, can't seem to learn your rules.

Baa Baa Black Sheep they're easy as can be. Practice til you get them right. Repeat after me! Always keep your hair in place.

—I try. It just won't stay.

Be sure to dress your very best.

—Every single day?

Take off all that make-up.

—You told me I looked grey.

For God's sake SMILE young lady.

—My braces are in the way.

Baa Baa Black Sheep you're very hard to train. Getting you to stand up straight is really quite a pain.

—Oh Sir, dear Sir, I try, I really do. I want so much to make you proud and be your perfect ewe. Perhaps if I crawled around and never stood up tall, I could hold my shoulders back and still appear quite small. But if that is not good enough to please you finally, I'll just turn myself into someone else, who is not a bit like me!"

Susanne was not at all amused. A few sessions later she told me that the story about my sister was one of the worst she'd ever heard. I felt vindicated. I wasn't crazy. They were.

My writer friend Anna often walked me to Susanne's. She was Italian, had been married, had a son, and was now smitten—the only word that works—with a much younger, French lesbian, self-centered, spoiled brat of a writer. As much as I disapproved whom Anna chose to give her heart—her lover was a leech and as far as I could see gave very little back to Anna—Anna disapproved of my going to therapy. Believed it would destroy whatever talent I had. "You'll come out a zombie," she'd say. "Look at you! You're certainly not getting better. You're even more depressed than when you started."

I tried to defend myself. Said that digging into stuff wasn't fun, but eventually it would help. Sometimes her accompanying me provided just enough energy to get me from my door to Susanne's. Often she'd wait so we could go for coffee together where she would inquire as to exactly what was said.

"She probably is trying to get therapy by osmosis," Susanne said.

"I don't know. She's adamant therapy is going to destroy whatever talent I have."

"And what do you think?"

I shrugged. "Munch could only paint pretty flowers after he emerged from the asylum."

"And what if he emerged able to live a full and happy life? Freud said the most important things we have are love and work. Are you able to do either now? Isn't that why you came here?"

"I thought you weren't a Freudian."

"I'm eclectic. Will use Freud when he applies."

One afternoon, I made Anna stay with me until Susanne buzzed me in so I could introduce them. I wanted them both to see how bright the other was and maybe even entice Anna herself into therapy. They hated each other on sight—the hello lasting less than a minute. Subtly Susanne weaned me off the friendship. Implied all the negativity was impeding our work. I wasn't even aware it was happening, but after a while I saw less and less of Anna until almost not at all.

———————————————

On another day, I arrived at Susanne's in a really good mood. It was one of the few times I'd passed the ambulances stationed outside of St. Vincent's hospital and had not wanted to climb in. A few minutes into the session she gently said she'd like me to see someone. Immediately my guard went up. I'd never heard her so tentative.

"Who?" I demanded.

"He's a psychopharmacologist. A lot of my patients go to him. I would like him to assess your mood swings. One day you're beyond depressed. Then you come in here all energized like today."

"Finally I'm in a good mood and this is when you think I need to see someone? That's crazy. Besides, I won't take drugs. Never did even when it was the thing to do—take enough for the asthma."

"We need to know how much of these swings are biologically based."

"What difference?"

"So we'll know how to treat it."

"You are treating it!"

"Margo, humor me please. Dr. Mas isn't the most empathetic

man you'll meet, but he is excellent at what he does."

I could feel my whole being lose the will to fight her. From early on going to doctors had been a way of life for me. I'm not sure which came first: my relishing the attention Mom paid to me when I got sick or my getting sick so Mom would pay attention. Rushing me to doctors could also have been my mother's way of relying on them to give me the attention she didn't have to give. (I would do the same with my cat, Mischa, taking him to the Vet at the slightest change in his behavior, knowing I never loved him as much as I loved Pablo.) Over time I learned how to make friends with the nurses, charm the doctors with humor, anything to deflect feeling intruded upon. (Probably why I fare better with male doctors than female ones—though it could also have to do with the time I lay on a gynecologist's table—I was twelve—with forceps inside me as two female GYNs attempted to stretch my insides so the menstrual blood could flow more freely—my mother and sister peering in from the door.)

"Margo!" Susanne cut into my thoughts. "I want you to go!"

I resigned myself to what seemed the inevitable and made the appointment. Mas sent me to NYU Hospital for testing. With electrodes attached to my head, white lights flashing before me, it felt more like science fiction than science. Before the results were in, Susanne wanted to know how I felt.

"Scared out of my wits."

"Why?"

"Because either way they win."

"Who?"

"The family, of course."

"How?"

"If the tests show there's something wrong with my brain, then they were right. I was born crazy. And if there's nothing wrong, then they were also right. I was just crazy. Either way, family wins; I lose."

The results came back. I was definitely not bipolar–though how they could tell from electrodes and lights I still can't figure out. And while the results showed a minor tendency to depression— and the upswings a form of self-medication—my asthma meds prevented Dr. Mas from prescribing an anti-depressant. Instead he ordered 5mg tablets of Ritalin to be taken as needed with a max of 30mgs per day. Frightened of becoming dependent, I was extremely stringent. When putting one foot in front of the other required more energy than I could muster, I'd call Susanne to check if it was alright to take even one pill. (I had no idea that at the time that Susanne was writing a book on the psychobiology of elation and depression which made her behave like someone wandering through a haunted house where every creek in a floor board sent off a warning sign that something unseen lurked around the corner.)

As much as I had avoided the art world, I felt obligated to attend Regina's husband opening. She had, after all, introduced me to Susanne and I'd known her husband, Herman Cherry, for years. Popping a Ritalin, I made my way to the gallery. Regina greeted me with a hug, and then quickly excused herself. I turned and saw she was heading over to a woman wearing an outfit that looked more appropriate for a camping trip than a New York art gallery: flannel shirt, jeans, and heavy hiking boots. She turned and I realized it was Susanne—she appeared so different from the woman who had sat across the room from me just a few days before. I watched them go off to a corner of the gallery and begin whispering to each other. I didn't know where to turn. A few minutes later,

Susanne came over, politely said hello and then left the gallery. I was certain they'd been talking about me.

Regina rushed back over. "Sorry about that. Her ex was here and I needed to give her a heads up."

At our next session, Susanne asked how I had felt seeing her there.

"Left out. Uncomfortable. Much like watching my mother and sister speak in Pig Latin so I wouldn't understand."

"I was afraid of that. Thought you might think we were whispering about you. We weren't."

"I know. Regina told me what you were talking about. But knowing didn't change how I felt. I still felt excluded."

A few days later Regina called to say she'd received a phone call from Susanne telling her not to discuss her with me, ever! It ended my contact with Regina for many years.

February '87

By now I was seeing Susanne two, sometimes even three times a week. I kept expecting some sort of breakthrough—a brilliant insight that would go off like a flash of lightning illuminating a path to a future. At home I wrote. Short pieces about my mother. Her death. My father. His death. Loss and more loss. Still in need of constant validation, I'd bring Susanne my latest attempts. She said she would read them while she was on vacation. Once again I had blocked out her schedule. At least this time I knew she would have me with her—on paper.

"My mom thought you had a gift for dialogue," she said upon her return.

I couldn't decide what to make of the comment. That I was lousy at everything else? That Susanne didn't have her own opinion? Of course, I'd wanted her to say what I'd written was brilliant.

"I had a teacher in college who thought I could write."

She looked annoyed. "I still cannot believe your parents didn't insist you stay there."

"Do you think my life would have been different?"

"Not the point! Your father should have insisted you get a degree. Jews have always had a respect for education."

I was horrified. Did she think her knowledge of Jews ran deeper than mine? What would she think if I lumped all Germans together? I kept quiet, afraid if I said anything it would cause a permanent rift.

The next few months were more of the same. A job as an extra here, seeing a friend there, and going to Susanne. Close to the end of June she asked what I planned to do for the summer.

"The same as I have been. Getting a job here and there. And thankfully seeing you. I've always found summers depressing. Everyone seems to leave town."

"I leave right before the July 4th weekend and will not be back until after Labor Day."

I went into shock. I had known shrinks took time off, usually in August, but an entire summer? She said she'd told me when I first came to her what her schedule was. Obviously, I'd chosen not to hear her. I managed to ask her where she went, frightened she'd say out of the country.

"To Amagansett. You can always call and if it's a real emergency, you can even come out for an appointment."

Her answer didn't allay my anxiety.

"Unless you'd like me to give you the name of someone you could call," she continued.

I reached for my inhaler. "What if we spend three days together? Maybe I'd have a breakthrough. I'll pay you whatever. Please!" I have no idea what I expected to break through to, but I desperately wanted the wall to come down that was blocking me from discovering what I could be or at least what direction to take.

"It doesn't work that way, Margo."

"But it could. I've read about shrinks who did that. Saw patients for more than an hour. Kept going until some moment of enlightenment was reached."

She just smiled and handed me a small pebble. "Keep this with you."

"Why?"

"It's something of mine. I picked it up off the beach. Hold onto it when the separation becomes too painful."

If I was desolate before she left in December and February, I was now in a full state of despair. The asthma attacks worsened. I took more Ritalin without a qualm.

In 1972 I had started keeping calendars on which I'd scrawl people's names, times of appointments, a date I wanted to remember, everything from Mom's death, to a friend's birthday and miscellaneous phone numbers. These large desk top sheets with their 2 x 3 inch boxes are a jumble of hastily written memory joggers. (I am told there are two types of people: those that save and those that toss. I toss. Most everything finds its way into the trash, from emails and newspapers the moment they're read, to tax statements as soon as it's legal to do so. I am anything but a saver. Thank-

fully, I kept these calendars for without them, this book couldn't
have been written.) What appalls is how many entries do not con-
jure up a face or an event. The word "disaster," written across an
entire row, tells me absolutely nothing. Yet I have no doubt that
the 3:30s and 2:45s clearly denote my visits to Susanne. July of '87
is mostly blank, but I clearly remember spending hours imagining
her entertaining friends, going to openings, shacking up with one
or more lovers. I would promise myself I wouldn't call her, then
break down with one excuse or another. The best ones having to
do with my mother's unveiling.

"Chuck doesn't want one. Even refuses to come." "I told him,
like you said that he doesn't have to." "He won't change his mind,
Susanne." "You won't believe this, but Marcia and Bud invited
everyone back to their home without asking me what I wanted." "I
tried what you said, but they're not changing their mind. For God's
sake, she was my mother, not theirs! And I don't give a flying fuck
if they live close to the cemetery. At least I should have been consulted!" Call after call after call.

In retrospect, I could have been more understanding of my
brother. He'd just spent months in a hospital close to death and
wanted to keep any thoughts of dying at bay. But as he hadn't
allowed me in to see him when he was sick, I was too hurt and
angry to care. In the end he came—my brother's threats so rarely
carried through. ("I'm going to get involved," he'd announced
one day at the height of the Civil Rights Movement. "*Meshugga*,"
my father retorted. "I am!" Chuck repeated. "You're not going to
march with the *Shvartzers*!" Dad using a word I detested. The two
kept at it, Chuck jabbing away knowing the response he would get.
The dispute with our father the only involvement with the Civil
Rights movement Chuck would ever have.)

My brother and I stood together as the rabbi said a prayer. I
could only see a blur of graves; Chuck noticed the dates on the
headstones. My sister's: 1964; my Dad: 1975 and now my Mom's:

1986.

"Look at that!" he whispered. "They're each eleven years apart."

None too tactfully I whispered back, "Should make you feel good, at least you don't have to worry for the next ten years."

"It's all yours," referring to the fourth grave we believed my brother-in-law to have purchased when my sister died. "I'm being cremated."

"Well so am I." I made sure to say this loud enough so Mom would hear. The last thing she'd want was to be stuck for eternity between Dad and me.

Out of spite I refused to go with the family to Marcia's, leaving with the Rabbi for coffee in her kitchen. I called Susanne to voice my sense of dislocation. "I should have gone to Marcia's, shouldn't I?"

"Margo! How many times do I have to tell you? There are no shoulds! If you didn't want to go with the family, you didn't have to go."

Her voice did not console. It was like calling Mom from camp—a topical anesthetic producing a brief moment of reassurance that quickly wore off leaving an intense ache.

Fall 1987

Labor Day came late extending the wait time for Susanne's return by a full week; I was on her steps at least a half hour early. When I got inside, I had nothing to say.

"Abandonment is painful, Margo," she said again. "And I've told you, I need time to truly refresh. To write. To come back to my patients with a clean head."

"Other shrinks do that in three weeks, for God's sake. But two months? What shrink does that? You're supposed to be the good enough mother! And may I remind you good enough mothers don't abandon their kids. Especially one who was left alone for months at a time."

"And may I remind you I expand heads, I don't shrink them. You are not going to get me angry by calling me a shrink even though you are well aware I don't approve of the term. Besides, the idea is for you to internalize the good-enough-mother so you don't have to be in close proximity to feel safe."

I took that to mean her role was to put salve on all my wounds. To listen to all the wrongs done to me and make up for them. It couldn't have been further from the truth. When exactly the first blows landed I can't be certain, but they came down like large hailstones chipping away at my very being. The first one fell a few sessions later when she accused me of never separating from my parents.

"Of course, I rebelled. That was my nickname. 'Margo, the Rebel.' Everyone called me that." Hadn't I been the only family member who had bucked the tide, gone against authority, turned my back on the mores of my parents' world? How could she go away for two months then accuse me of not being the one thing I'd built my life upon?

"Margo, a rebel is someone who separates, goes off, fully leaves home. A person who continues to react in rebellion is still very much attached." She was opening and closing her hands as if there was a rubber band around them. "You didn't stay in California. You didn't stay in Italy. You never left the family. This was you!" And with that she snapped her hands shut with a large clap entwining her fingers.

"I moved out of their house, for God's sake, to an apartment in the same city when no one in our circle did that!" My voice now up an octave. "Other people my age in those years, from my milieu, didn't dare."

"You could have gone to another city."

"Who the hell leaves New York if one wants a career in the arts?"

"Or stayed in California. Or Italy. You chose not to each time after only two months. You might have been at camp."

The blow hit home. My forays away had always lasted all but two months—the same as sleep away camp to which I'd been sent at age three. Well, to be honest, three and a half—six months does make a difference at that age. And yes, a governess had gone with me that first summer, but I'd been on my own after that. Still, for her to bring that up when I was still in pain from the separation…

"As I said, Margo, you could have gone somewhere else and stayed."

"Like you did coming here? Leaving Frankfurt for New York makes a lot of sense. New York for Oshkosh does not."

"We're not talking about me."

"I bet."

For the first time since her return I was actively engaged. In the next session she ripped into my father.

"Stop holding him up as all powerful. What did he achieve? Was he a doctor? A scientist? A philosopher? No! He was a merchant!" her voice filled with the same disdain as when my father demanded a waiter take back food not up to his standards—which was every time we dined out.

"For God's sake, Susanne. He was self-made. Came here with nothing from a Russian *shtetl*. No education. No mother—she'd died giving birth to him. I think he did damn well for himself."

"You've made my point. He knew his underpinnings weren't

there. That's what grandiosity is. A façade built on nothing." And then she went for the jugular. "Grandiose narcissistic parents produce grandiose narcissistic children."

I fell back against the wall as if slapped across the face. It was one thing to label my parents narcissists. But to include me? "I'm not narcissistic, Susanne," I gasped.

She jumped up and reached for a book from a shelf. "Write down the title and get it," she ordered handing me a piece of paper and pen.

"Why can't you lend it to me?"

"I don't lend out my books. You can go to the library or a bookstore."

I left the office reeling. Not only had she called me grandiose, but now she wouldn't even share a book from her shelf. Still, dutifully I made my way to Barnes & Noble. They didn't have it, so I went home, called her and got the name of a bookstore that carried books on psychology and headed there where I plunked down the $50, aghast at the price. At home I started reading not expecting to understand one word. Instead, by the next session, I came in with pencil-marked, paper-clipped pages eager for her to elucidate.

"Was the excitement I experienced at having understood some of what I read, narcissistic?"

"No, it's perfectly legitimate to feel proud of an achievement as long as the pride doesn't extend beyond the specific accomplishment."

"Did my need to perform fall under exhibitionism?"

"Yes, but that's too simplistic an answer."

I opened the book to page 10 and thrust it in front of her. "Am I like Kohut's patient M?" It was a paragraph that had hit home.

"Do you see similarities?"

I nodded. "I can be working on something, a piece of dialogue or a scene, and suddenly every nerve ending feels on fire, as if my body can no longer contain itself. When it happens, I think I'm going to jump out of my skin. The emotions get so huge I have to get away, walk it off, call someone. By the time I calm down, the muse is gone. I go back to work, but without a spark. When I was sculpting, it happened non-stop."

"It's the ego soaring out of control. It has to do with a lack of basic self-esteem. In order to feel good about yourself—good enough is never good enough—you have to feel brilliant and ..."

"My dad's need for a genius!"

"Meaning?"

"Dad believed if you were a genius you didn't need to study and if you were less than one, you shouldn't bother."

"In other words, you had to be a genius or you were nothing? That had to make it very difficult to learn anything."

"It was. Still, Dr. B assured me I wasn't an idiot. The word she actually used was brilliant." I don't know what possessed me to bring that up. A need for validation? For affirmation? It is certainly not what I got back.

"She did what? And we looked up to her!" Susanne's voice filled with visceral horror.

I didn't know what to address first. The fact that she obviously didn't think I was brilliant or that she'd known Dr. B. The age difference had to be enormous. Besides, Dr. B was an accredited MD; Susanne of the PH.D school. I opted for the safer of the two.

"How did you know her?"

"Met her at meetings. She was one of the few women who had

made it in the closed all-male community of psychiatrists. I can't believe she would tell a patient with grandiose tendencies that she was brilliant. It's disastrous."

I hated the sound of it. Of me being grandiose. Of Bookie screwing up. "I'm sure she was just trying to let me know I didn't have a low IQ. I told you, Dr. B worked hard to make me believe I wasn't born an idiot."

For years I'd put down therapists who practiced without an MD license as not being educated enough, and it was Dr. B who had come to their defense saying some were doing very good work. Now here I was with one of them defending Dr. B.

"I mean it was she who tried to get me to study drawing and sculpture. Tried to get me over the hump of thinking I had to be a 'natural.'"

"And you don't send a patient with grandiose tendencies further into the arts. You keep them moored to something far more concrete!"

Obviously my work with Dr. B had only fueled a fire already out of control. I searched for something to salvage from those years. "She did try to stop me from leaving my job. I really think she panicked when I did."

"And rightly so!"

I made one last attempt to salvage any sense of self. "She once asked why I couldn't sculpt and be married to an Ambassador at the same time. Entertain the elite like a woman she knew. I hated the thought. Part of me must have known it was grandiose thinking on her part." I expected kudos from Susanne at my being able to connect the dots. Again, not what I got.

"Perhaps. Or your reaction could have stemmed from something else entirely."

"Like what?"

"Your aversion to marriage, to commitment, to playing a similar role to your mother's."

Obviously there was no winning. I shut up.

"Where are you now?" she asked. "You appear to have left the room."

"Just remembering a therapist I went to a while ago. He was supposed to fix things after ten sessions. I lasted only one."

Susanne threw her legs off the ottoman as if ready to spring into action. "Why?" she demanded.

"He told me to close my eyes and imagine myself in a room. I put myself in the loft. Then he asked what I was wearing, I told him my long wrap skirt, sandals, and top. Mom used to call it my hippy-yippy outfit. Then he said to imagine someone in the room with me. Asked who it was. I told him a man, but I didn't know who. He told me to walk towards him. Suddenly I couldn't breathe. I felt I was going to be sucked up like into a vacuum. I got the hell out of there. Left and never went back ... Just want you to know my dad never abused me."

"I didn't say he had."

"No, but you were thinking that."

"Me or you?"

I wished the session over. I'd had enough.

"Me or you, Margo?"

"Okay, he was seductive. But that's not abuse."

"Depends. You're keeping something back."

"It was nothing. Just a moment. That's all it was. I'd gone into their room for something or other. Who knows? Dad was in bed in his pajamas, Mom resting on the chaise. I don't know why as he never had before, but suddenly Dad begged me to get into bed with him and cuddle. I thought it crazy. Laughed and told him no, but Mom began to plead with me to do so, to make him happy, give him a hug. I gave in. Climbed under the covers, but within seconds feeling his body next to mine I recoiled, jumped out of the bed and ran from the room. He was so hurt. So angry. Dr. B was furious when I told her." I unclasped my hands from around my body where I had held them throughout the telling.

"How old were you?"

"Sixteen or seventeen. Somewhere around then." I thought Susanne would dig into this deeper. That we would get into my relationships with men, but she stayed silent. Then,

"Again, now where are you?"

"I was just thinking how I'd rather be seated where you are than here."

"Are you interested in becoming a therapist?"

That wasn't what I meant. I had just wanted the roles switched. Craved to know what she knew. Get this process over and done with. I hated the limbo of it all. "Do you think I could be?" I asked, not caring one way or another.

"Yes. I do." She was serious.

For an instant my ego soared. "Really?"

"Really."

Then it collapsed. "Can't."

"Why not?"

"Credits. Would need to finish college. Then get a Masters.

Christ! And then a PHD. I'd be over a hundred and a pauper." I left out that studying was never a favored pastime of mine. Besides, I'd been a starving artist for over eighteen years; I did not relish the thought of many more spent leading a paltry existence.

"There are colleges that give life credits. It would be worth looking into."

"Even so, do you know how many years that would take? Just to get through college and a Masters? Forget about the Ph.D."

"You don't need a Ph.D."

"Of course I do. The last thing I'd want is to be is an undereducated, mediocre, average shrink!"

"And what's wrong with average?" she said, jumping up from her chair like an exclamation mark.

I couldn't believe she'd say such a thing. "To be average is to be nothing, for God's sake."

"Well, I'm average and I do not consider myself nothing." She moved to turn on a corner lamp as the room had darkened.

Was she fishing for a compliment? She had degrees from Frankfurt University and Columbia, had been published in Germany and the U.S., ran a Referral Service, taught at the New School, had a roster of patients—not to mention she owned a home in the Hamptons and half a brownstone in New York.

"Like hell you're average!" I snapped. Who the hell was she kidding? She was now in front of her shelves with their thousands of books—a clear substantiation of what I was saying.

"With my background and history, I'm average."

"What's your background?"

"Grandparents and parents who were artists and professors."

I sank. All I had was a peddler on my father's side and a printer on Mother's. "On a scale of 1 to 100 where's average?"

"Between 70 and 85."

I must have turned pale, because her tone softened.

"There's nothing wrong with a good bottle of table wine, Margo," she said as if inviting me to dine.

"If you're table wine, where the hell does that leave me?" I'd immediately flashed back to a French friend's only slightly camouflaged look of revulsion when I'd arrived with an inexpensive bottle of table wine for what she said would be a pot luck dinner. It turned out to be no more than some bread and cheese and even then, the wine was rejected.

"My grandfather was published in sixteen languages. I only one. For my education and background, I am average. I am not Freud. I am not Kohut."

At least by this time I knew who Kohut was.

Before the month was out, Susanne had me sending for my college transcripts as well as making an appointment at the Empire State Board that gave credits for life experience. I wasn't enamored of the prospect. It seemed a long, thankless, grueling road. The man I met with confirmed my suspicions. With only one year of college—most of that producing only theater credits—and only four years at an ad agency, it would take way too many years to get a degree. Shrinkdom was out.

Frightened I would spend all of Mom's money and be a bag lady out on the street, I went to work for a friend from high school who ran a corporate gift buying business—having turned her desire for material things into a money making machine. If I had been miserable before, my sense of self plummeted as she relegated me to her back room wrapping packages for shipment. She found fault with everything, treated me and her other employees deplorably, and talked down to all including her partner.

A few days before my fiftieth birthday Bud's wife Marcia called to ask how I planned to celebrate.

"No plans."

"Would you like to go for dinner?"

I asked if it could be just the two of us. With Susanne away, I craved an in-depth, personal conversation—my brother-in-law not one to dig into psyches.

"I'm sure Buddy wouldn't mind if that's what you'd like."

It was. Just a one-on-one, as low key as possible. Of course, I expected Marcia, an MSW, to be a proponent of therapy. But over dinner when she asked how my therapy was going, I sensed a strong antipathy which I immediately took to be towards Susanne. Who could blame her? Clearly I appeared worse than when I started. (It would be years before I'd learn that Marcia was wary of almost all therapists. I'd go so far as to say she had little respect if any for the therapeutic process itself.)

"It's fine," I lied. "Difficult, But fine." I was so afraid if I opened up about how I felt, Susanne, my lifeline, would be denigrated, or at the very least, undermined by doubt.

I'm sure the food was fine, though I have no memory of what we ordered, but then I can count on one hand memorable meals I've had. There was no cake, no candles—only my silent despair. So for all intents and purposes my 50th birthday could have been held at a Trappist abbey—come to think of it, that might have been far more interesting.

Part II

*I climb on the rock in my party dress and sing God Bless
America at the top of my lungs.*

*I am two and a half. My father smiles;
the guests applaud.*

*Years later I ask Mom where was my rock and she points to a
stone all of four inches high
with a circumference of no more than ten inches.*

I am in disbelief.

*Had memory warped reality? Had it grown larger in my
mind's eye as I did?*

It is what confronts me with every word I write.

The Family before I Came Along

When You Grow Up, what Will You Be?

Whatever Concentrates All Eyes On Me!

My poor siblings. There they were, hitting their teenage years and along comes a rival for their parents' attention. One who, according to my mother, suffered from colic. Well, that's not exactly how she put it.

"I have no idea if you were allergic to milk. All I know is that your father walked you on the nurse's night out! You had colic, you know." Then, after a sigh of great weight, "You never understood how much he loved you. Why you rejected him I'll never know."

To which I retorted, "Well, good thing the colic cleared up before I was six months old or I'd have been out of luck," which led to Mom's,

"Don't start!"

And my, "I didn't. You did." Mom and I could pick up conversations as if they had never been laid down.

We were both alluding to when I was six months old and my father walked into my room with a friend to show me off and I burst out crying—a loud bawling cry. His friend teased him with, "Hey, Jay, she mustn't like you" causing my overly sensitive father to walk out of my life for the next year and a half. By the time he came round, I wasn't prepared to accept him, setting up a pattern that would continue until right before he died.

"Make me a promise," he whispers. He is all pallid skin and fleshless bones.

"What is it," I ask. I'm afraid he'll make me promise to move in with my mom.

He repeats his request. I need to know what I'm promising. We repeat

this dance until finally, he says, "Promise me when you're ready you'll quit smoking."

I'm surprised at his "when you're ready." He'd never given me options before. Hell, I might never be ready. I am already up to four packs a day. But when you're ready? "Sure, Dad. I promise."

"And don't become a lush like your brother," he adds, for the moment sounding like his old all-powerful self.

I laugh. "Couldn't. I fall asleep after two drinks."

Silence.

Then, "Do you love me?"

"Of course!" I say.

"That's all I ever wanted to hear," he whispers and closes his eyes.

He did not say he loved me. But hey, he died in peace. (Well, he would have if the bloody nurse hadn't withheld his morphine afraid she'd be sued for murder.)

As I'd explained to Susanne, I was never physically abused; there was plenty of food—after all we were in the food business—and I was properly dressed whether I wished to be or not. I also had my own room—at least until I was sixteen when we moved to the East Side and I had to share it with my father. Not in the conjugal sense, but as they'd kept the décor of the red room intact—only changing the sofa to a bed made to look like a sofa—on nights they entertained, I would move to one of the two maid's rooms so Dad could play cards in mine with his buddies.

Friends were hard to come by. The children of my parents' friends were my siblings' ages, my cousins were mostly older, and my parents paid someone off so I could travel across the park to attend P.S. 6, one of the better public grammar schools in the city. This meant that while the other kids congregated after school, had playdates and the like, the minute the bell rang I was whisked back across the park by a governess or nurse maid, lest I be found out and expelled for being illegally there.

Camp didn't produce friends either. Up to age 11 when my braces were attached, I was a thumb sucker. I also wet my bed until age 7. Add to the mix my total lack of athletic ability—I was always the last one picked for a team—I'd come home pleading not to be sent back. Most years my mother would find a different one—each a mirror image of the last. I can still reel off their names in the order of my attendance just as I used to do to anyone who would listen, as if sticking a pin into a voodoo doll created in my parents' image. "Lenore, Lenore, Lenore, Kinnikineck, Greylock Greylock and so on. To be fair, morose children do not attract and I certainly wasn't the happiest of kids.

At Camp

Around age ten, my parents found an alternative: a farm camp called Journey's End. Whether it was for emotionally disturbed children, talented ones, or a combination of both, I will never know. I adored it, but sadly, it only lasted two summers after the owner wrote my mother that all I needed was love.

"What did you tell her?" Mom cried, referring to Edith the camp owner. "That we're ogres? You were a love child, for God's sake! Did you tell her that?"

I never understood why I was called a love child, An expression Mom used when she suspected me of saying I wasn't wanted. Considering a few years later I learned she'd sought an abortion when pregnant with me, it made even less sense. Anyway, I was yanked out of Journey's End, had to go to one more sports camp and then, finally, permitted to attend ones that focused on music and art where I studied voice, dance and Musical Theater. Always in need of adult attention—one night, before a show for the parents—one that mine didn't attend—I swallowed a bunch of diuretic pills meant to help alleviate some of my menstrual difficulties. Temporary dizziness was all the pills produced and I went on stage after another camper's father, a doctor who saw through my feeble attempt, administered his own form of therapy, "Get on the stage and show them what you can do!" I sang my part doing so as provocatively as I could, coming on at fifteen as if my virginity was long gone. Forget that I'd never even been kissed by a boy, gone out on a date, or heard sex discussed home. Anything with even a hint of a double entendre would cause my mother to blush which meant, for all her protestations to the contrary, she'd understood the joke.

Words of wisdom from my mother:

"A woman should be a Madonna in the living room and a whore in the bedroom." (This could have been in response to an outfit I'd bought she thought too revealing.)

"A woman has to know when to tell her husband things. Timing is all

important." (I had asked her why she was hiding her new clothes in the back of the closet.)

And: *"Women have to give 75%, dear—The men only 25. That's just the way it is."* She said this as she packed up the most beautiful gown I'd ever seen. It was pink satin, with a full skirt, gathered up on one side and, tucked in its folds, a large deep red silk rose. Mom had bought it for my brother's wedding. The gown she had worn to my sister's matronly and ugly. Mom had put on the pink satin and danced around the apartment. I had never seen her so beautiful or so happy. Then Dad came home.

"You look like a floozy!" he spat out in disgust. "Send it back. You're not going in that!"

She pled. I pled. She caved—tears welling up in both our eyes— the rims of hers turning red. That's when she explained her 75/25 ratio. I vowed then never to marry; the price clearly way too high.

I lived for approval. Whether it was my mother's praise after I completed the centerpiece for one of their many dinner parties, or the applause from the crowd at my parents' 25th Wedding Anniversary party after I sang The Girl that I Married, or during talent night at the Nautilus Hotel—where my parents went for the summer and I would join them before and after camp. Put me in front of an audience—the larger the better—and I'd sing my heart out.

Taking a Bow at Parents' 25th

There did come a time, however, when I decided I would no longer perform for my parents' friends—I am certain to their great relief. "I'm not going in there," I told my father. My voice lowered so the company in the living room couldn't hear. "Not!" Bad enough I had to dress up just to say hello.

My father's eyes filled with rage—Mom's pleading with me not to cause a scene.

"But they're waiting!"

"Not my problem. I am not singing. I'm twelve!"

Life upon the Wicked Stage

My infatuation with the musical stage had begun when I was four and my mother took me to see The Merry Widow. From then on, I went with her to a Broadway musical once almost every year.

I've lost the order—and sadly tossed out all The Playbills—but after The Merry Widow came Oklahoma, Peter Pan, Carousel, Out of This World, Mame, Guys and Dolls, South Pacific, The Most Happy Fella, and Paint Your Wagon. (I still think of Paint Your Wagon as one of the most underrated shows. For those readers interested, get a recording of the original Broadway version and pay particular attention to How Can I Wait, a song I often sang to myself whenever desperate for time to pass. It is perfection. I was in a producer's office when Lerner, the lyricist came in. I mentioned Paint Your Wagon as my favorite of his shows. He said he agreed and said it had never gotten its due.) The last shows Mom and I went to together were A Chorus Line and The Fantasticks which I'd loved from the moment it first came out and one she'd never seen—my father refusing to go to Greenwich Village where it was playing. Each year there would be another wonderful musical whose characters' lives meant more to me for weeks after than those around me.

Mom chose Riverdale Country Day in the Bronx for junior and high school. In those days the Boys and Girls schools were separate—the sexes only getting together for Glee Club, attending intra-mural games, and on the buses that shuttled us from the city up to the school and back. I hated when we pulled into the Boys School to change to the bus that would take us home. It was a meat market and I the lean burger they all passed on. I receded into the background as much as possible not even showing up for class pictures. Nose job or not, there were still those fangs and braces.

Then, in our senior year, I auditioned for the female lead in Finian's Rainbow. I am certain I got the part at the urging of my singing teacher—the woman who had introduced me to Menotti. She and the head of music at the Boy School had begun to date and it was he who would be directing. As we had moved only the year before, I could identify with the role of Sharon. A young woman torn from the home she loved by a father who was seeking a pot of gold. As I sang How are things in Glocca Morra? all my feel-ings of loss emerged. Sharon's weeping willow was my dogwood tree I'd watched from my bedroom window overlooking the park; the laddie with the twinkling eye, Eddie our elevator man who, when no one else was around, had let me control the lever; the brook that went from Donny Cove through Killybegs, Kilkerry and Kildare, the entire West Side. My father attended the first performance along with my favorite aunt who told him how good I was. For the next few months my father wore my success like a medal on his lapel.

My affair with sculpture also had its roots at Riverdale. I was 13. Our teacher, Peter Haywood, came once a week. He was tall and elegant with long fingers that directed ours. We would sit around a large table, a mound of Plasticine on a wooden board in front of each of us and model the clay. I knew what I wanted to make: A Washer Woman. I put her in a dress, with her legs folded beneath her, sitting back on her heels. I had one hand rest on her thigh; the other hold a scrub brush as she wiped her brow with the back of her hand. Here too, desperate for Mr. Haywood's attention, I called him over with every mark I made. He gave it patiently. He showed us how to make a mold and cast our work—a delicate proposition. My relief was overwhelming when my washer woman emerged intact. Haywood entered our pieces in a national contest and I received a tiny key on a chain from Scholastic. (I still have the key though where the sculpture is, I have no idea.) My mother prized the piece, showed it off even though she would have preferred I'd chosen a more elegant subject; perhaps a reclining woman lounging on a chaise. But my attachment was to my beloved Tessie. I iden-tified with her whose hands actually looked worked to the bone. In Art Class (not to be confused with Peter Haywood's sculpture sessions) I drew huge women on three by ten feet sheets of brown paper. I would roll the paper onto the floor, then reach down with chalks and draw one after another. Were they me? Probably. Or what I longed to be. Strong. Present. Visible to all. As they were way past the size deemed appropriate to hang in a student show, they were never shown. Many years later I would draw even larger, more voluptuous women—for the record I am thin boned with minimal flesh. They were bought by a dance company to be used as scenery. Whether they, or the company, still exist here too I have no idea.

Somewhere between ten and twelve I also wrote songs. Terrible terrible songs. The lyrics I can remember much to my embarrassment. "Did you know know know that down in Mexico there's a senorita named Dynamo. She drives the boys completely wild when she does the Mexican rumba." I won't bore you with any of the others except one that from my vantage point now strikes me as slightly sad. "Can't you believe in me, is that so hard to do, I never meant …" I know it was my version of a love song, but I have to wonder for whom those lyrics were actually meant.

I rarely if ever sang unless I had an audience. Nor did my hands itch to draw. I didn't sketch or doodle. But then, it didn't matter. Drawing and sculpting were sidelines. I was going to be a star and perform on the Broadway stage. It never dawned on multi-talented me that I could sing, dance, draw, sculpt—all at the same time for the sheer pleasure of it all. Perhaps it was a form of self-protection. If I didn't succeed at one, I could say it was because I really was something else. A dancer who sang; a singer who danced; an actor who sculpted; a sculptor who acted. Oh! And of course, a song writer if things got really rough.

Clearly only a college with a theater program would do. There were few choices: Northwestern, Syracuse, Boston U. The more prestigious ones like Sarah Lawrence I didn't even consider—even Northwestern seemed out of reach as I'd gone through school believing I had an IQ of 67. This misconception originated with my mother telling me I'd been rejected by Hunter for their kindergarten program. Where the 67 came from, I have no idea. This underestimation of my mental faculties was not helped when Riverdale switched from the A-F grading system to Pass/Fail meaning I never knew where I actually stood. The number hung like a thick layer of gauze between me and my studies. When you don't think you're smart, everything gets filtered through a negative haze. Desperate to have the correct answers on a test, I would do mental cartwheels around every question. Just how convoluted my thought processes could be became excruciatingly clear when I was well into my twenties. I was having my morning coffee, reading the NY Times before heading to work, when a headline stopped me cold. I don't remember its exact language, but it had to do with some ridiculous amount of money having been spent on the testing of nine year olds. The word "test" was more than enough to cause me to break out into a cold sweat, but it was the sample questions in the article that provoked a full-blown panic attack. My entire body shaking, I forced myself to take the quiz. I never got past the first question with its two accompanying pictures. One had a glass of water with a rock in it; the other, the glass of water with two halves of the rock beside it. Any thinking person wouldn't have even needed to read the question to know the answer: two halves make a whole. But not me! Here's how my mind worked:

If I remove the rock, I will lose water, but if I cut the rock in two, then I will lose grains of the rock, then again ... well you get the idea. The possibilities endless, needless to say, I flunked the test over coffee at home.

Shortly after I confessed my low IQ to Dr. B, she sent me back "across the street" to ask Mom why Hunter had rejected me. And voila! It had nothing to do with my mental capacity. Simply, I had not been emotionally mature enough at three years old to get admitted—forget kindergarten started at age five.

My mother and I were supposed to go to Syracuse for my college interview, but on the day we were to fly, Mom didn't feel well and I went alone. I had never flown before and wanted to cancel, but Mom said to go, that I'd be fine. When I got to the campus a young woman directed me to the main building, adding that before I left I should definitely visit Sims 4. "It's the New Yorker's dorm," she said. Strangely there had been no interview set up. Confused as to why I was there, and with time to kill before my return flight, I wandered around until I found my way to the dorm she's suggested. Two young women sat on the steps outside—one turned out to be Suzanne Pleshette, the other her friend Judith (her last name gone from memory.) They were both adamant that I not attend Syracuse. "It's the sticks here!" they said in unison. "We're leaving as soon as we can." When Judith learned my last name she said my father had been engaged to her mother and had taken back the engagement ring at the last minute—a story confirmed by my mother once I arrived home. "He was a bon vivant, your father." Mom said with obvious pride. "He gave that ring away a lot before he met me."

I ended up going to Boston University, partly because it wasn't Syracuse, partly because my brother-in-law's family lived in Brookline, Mass. and could provide me with a home away from home if needed. But mostly because a dental surgeon, who said he could replant the fangs—still in my mouth—practiced in Boston. (Turns out he was looking for a test case. He'd had some success with three and four year olds, but never someone at 17 and warned us it might not work. The implants failed; two false teeth were put in their place; my parents paid.)

The first play produced at BU that year was Arthur Miller's The Crucible. I auditioned and got the part of Elizabeth Proctor, one of the three leads. The director, Peter Kass, cast another freshman, Susan Harrison, as Abigail. It was probably typecasting all around. I could be judgmental, up-tight and prudish—certainly inept where men were concerned whereas Susan was all sex, and known for her wild escapades on campus. (She either left school early for Hollywood or was asked to leave. One day she was simply gone.)

"Get her off me. She's suffocating me," Russell, the actor playing John

Proctor yells out—lines not in the script.

Kass tells him, "That's how you're supposed to feel."

I feel awkward and ashamed. Yes, it's Goody Proctor being rejected, but I am her. Am I so repulsive?

Surprisingly, or maybe not so, I saved the review: "The three female leads were handled by 17-year-old freshmen. Margo Krasne as Proctor's wife was ideally cast as the cold-unbending woman who drove the farmer to lechery. Exercising admirable restraint she carried off the role with precise exactness." According to the review, we received 9 curtain calls.

David Pressman, a blacklisted director, headed Boston University's School of the Theater. His claim to fame: he'd directed Grace Kelly in The White Swan for TV. He and Kass had an unspoken rivalry. When it became clear that Kass had a "thing" for Harrison; Pressman took me on as his protégé. He decided I should leave college and head towards a professional school in New York. My ego stroked, I didn't argue going so far as to arrange a meeting at my parents' home during our Spring break.

I sit perched on the back of my father's red chair, my stomach in knots while my father presses David as to whether or not I possess talent. "I mean real talent!" he demands to know.

I can't believe he'd ask such a thing. Hadn't he brought me out to sing in front of company from the age of two? Knew of my successes in Boston—not to mention Finian's. And now, he's asking my acting teacher if I have talent? I bite my lip and wait for David's response.

"She walked off with all the leads, Mr. Krasne. No freshman does that."

Pressman was small: 5' 3" at the most, whereas Dad stood a little over 5' 8"—those 5 inches no doubt helping to bolster his sense of superiority. I can still see them, both men holding tumblers, most likely filled with scotch, standing only a few feet from each other.

Two Russian immigrants like cocks in a village pit. Only this pit was our living room with a thick piled white carpet from China on which no blood (or anything else) could be spilt.

Dad keeps going at it. "You know it's a lousy life. What happens if she fails? Will you take care of her?"

"She won't fail. You have one talented girl there, Mr. Krasne!"

I jammed my teeth into my bottom lip afraid I might break his streak if I uttered a word. My mother sat on the celadon green silk sofa a spectator to the entire scene. I could see she was torn. I knew that part of her wished I would stay in college if for no other reason than to give her peace and quiet as she spent much of her time when I was home acting as referee between my father and me—and the school David was recommending was back in New York. The other part of her found it easier to give into my wants—even going to bat for me—rather than to continue to listen to my insistent pleas. All of which she found exhausting.

"College will only hold her back, Mr. Krasne,"

Oh how conflicted my father must have been—he who had come to the U.S. with so little education. Yes he probably attended a Yeshiva as a child in Russia and a night school English language class as required if he wished citizenship when he arrived here in 1917. But basically he picked up most of what he knew from watching movies. If Cary Grant appeared in a dinner jacket, Dad had one the next week. If he learned that a successful businessman frequented a particular restaurant, we were there soon after. Besides, if I were truly talented, he wouldn't have to spend his money on lessons. I would be discovered.

"Did Caruso study? No! He was a natural!"

"Even the greats study, Mr. Krasne."

The back and forth between the two men continued until David went for the coup de gras.

"First the Neighborhood Playhouse under Sanford Meisner. And from there, Mr. Krasne, Broadway!"

In a flash it was over. Instant stardom was what Dad craved. (My father looked down on actors—or anyone in the arts for that matter—unless they were famous.) He would also save on an extra year of school as well as three years of room and board. So my mother resigned herself to my moving back home and two more years of warfare. If I'd been honest with myself, my trajectory would have been quite different. I hadn't loved being Goody Proctor—only the accolades I received after the performance. I'd been uncomfortable inhabiting another's body, being spurned by Russell—no matter what the character called for. I loved performing not acting. There's a huge difference—no camouflage unless wanted. But I'd fought hard for my chance at stardom so to the Playhouse I would go. There was no turning back.

The Playhouse: No Funhouse

From the opening day of The Playhouse I lived under the spell of Sanford Meisner. I was not alone. He was our God, gliding across the classroom, pelvis forward, chin slightly raised, always with dramatic flair. His theatrical elocution made his speech sound slightly foreign. Was I conscious of the similarities between Sandy and my father? Doubtful. In so many ways they were light years apart. My father loved musicals; Sandy professed to hate them. He put musical theater down along with Uta Hagen (and any of us whom he thought acted in her fashion,) Hollywood, and "indicators"—those actors who showed what they were supposed to feel rather than actually experienced the emotion. My father, on the other hand, would go into raptures hearing Al Jolson sing Swanee or Eddie Fisher Oh My Papa. "Now that's singing! That's what a

singer should sound like!" The implication: if you couldn't belt it
out like them, you couldn't sing. That Caruso started lessons at 16,
I wouldn't learn until many years later.

I am not sure that underneath Sandy didn't agree with my
father's "genius" premise. I often watched him leave alone those
students he felt would go on to "make it." And while he also paid
scant attention to those he thought were not worth his efforts, his
hands-off policy on future stars like Robert Duval reinforced my
fears that my father was right.

Both men were rulers of their domain. Impeccable dressers, they
roamed their halls stunning those around into silence. Dad in his
Sulka suits and hand-painted ties (painted by a woman with one
arm in a shop in the back of a hotel.) Sandy with a large handker-
chief flaring out of his breast pocket, his suit fabric a tad bit shinier
than my father's. The two men were of the same height with similar physiques. Both had voices warm and enticing one moment,
filled with disgust the next. And they both possessed the ability
to be simultaneously seductive and withholding—their eyes could
turn from a twinkling come-hither look to one of fury in a lightning second. (I would confuse this dangling of great things to
come as a sign of love for years, both as the teased and the teaser. In
my mind, any form of attention was better than no attention at all.)

Classes with Sandy and his assistants were spent in exercises
meant to rid us of any affectations and bad habits we may have
acquired. We were to find our internal truth. Dissecting of a character's truth wasn't where we were to focus. We were to pay attention to the other actor's response and our surroundings. Stanislavs-
ki's Method according to Meisner! I kept my love of musical theater
to myself, frightened he would do to me what he did to another
girl in class. Out of the blue, with no warmup, no accompaniment,
he made her get up and sing a song from a musical. Then he denigrated her and any of us who wished to perform in them. (She
would go on to be a well-known soap opera star.)

While the other students worked on voice modulation and projection—I learned to pronounce an "r." (Much time was spent in rehearsals of The Crucible finding a replacement for the rabbit I was to serve my husband as "wabbit" wouldn't do. It wasn't easy. Everything we could come up with from squirrel to muskrat had an "r." We settled for pigeon whether they were used for food then or not. Since Kass also added a drumroll to cover the sound of my cracking knees while I slowly sunk to the floor as the final curtain descended—all highly dramatic but incredibly wrong for the time—I figured if a drum could be heard while John Proctor hung by his neck, I could offer up a pigeon for dinner.) I spent hours at home reciting into a tape recorder, "the ragged rabbit ran around the rugged rock" only to hear back, "the wagged wabbit wan awound ..." It took six months until I could hear as I spoke what others had been hearing all along. Only then was I able to learn how to manipulate my tongue to make an "r." (To this day if I am overly tired or emotional, out will come the old "w". Trust me, "You weally arh cwazy" does not serve one well in the midst of an argument.)

In fencing class, Alvin Epstein would have us stand in the *en garde* position, epee in hand, arm extended, turning the tips of the blade around an imaginary penny for what seemed like forever. Epstein would saunter in, slowly collect his gear, and only when our arms were at the point of giving out, did he begin class. I won all my matches not because of any fencing prowess. Suspense has always been my enemy producing overwhelming anxiety. As I waited in position for the match to begin, the tension would build within me to such an extent that when Alvin said, "Start!" I'd let out an almost primal scream, frightening the hell out of my opponents, causing them to fall back behind the line.

We studied choreography with Louis Horst, ballet with Pearl Lang and modern dance with Jane Dudley—an extraordinary Graham dancer and teacher—as well as other members of the

Graham company. But the moments that were magical, the ones where we saw what true genius was like, was when Martha herself came to teach.

"Fall to the floor leaving an imprint like a cat in the sand."

"Move like butterflies in the wind,"

And my favorite—"Take the dare!" Her voice impelling us into mid-air as we leapt across the floor. "Take the dare!"

No matter how many books have been written about her, not one captures what it was like to be in her presence. She was unearthly and I quickly became her acolyte as well as Sandy's.

Meanwhile, life at home was anything but easy. Dad and I could butt heads over the simplest matter: not running to give him a kiss when he came home, or my walking around the apartment with curlers in my hair, or racing from my room to the bathroom in the hall in my slip. Even the hour I got out of bed became a bone of contention. Sleep and I had never been on friendly terms. It might have started with governesses requiring I recite that dreadful bedtime prayer, "Now I lay me down to sleep" when I figured out if I stayed awake I could ward off death; or straining to hear the sounds of my parents' parties desperate to be with the grownups rather than alone in my room. Even at camp when naps were enforced, I feigned sleep. By the time I was in my late teens, I had trained myself to need very little which did not please Dad at all.

For as long as I can remember Dad served Mom breakfast in bed. He'd put up the coffee in the percolator, take out the cottage cheese, rolls, jam and set them up on the two breakfast bed trays the cook had prepared the night before. Then he'd carry Mom's tray into their room after which he'd return with his, climb back into one of their twin beds to partake of the morning repast. (When I described this to a friend, he wanted to know who had breakfasted with me. I'd never even entertained the thought that someone should have.) On school days it would be expected I'd be up, but on weekends when I'd hear Dad's slippered feet pass my door, I'd run from my room to meet him only to be berated for not being asleep. "Normal girls stay in bed on weekends. Go back to bed!" What started out as a desire on my part for contact quickly turned a test of wills with my making certain never to sleep past seven o'clock no matter how late I'd gone to bed. (Mother often said Dad and I were more alike than not.)

I bristled at my father's inquiring whether or not a friend was "An M.O.T.?" (Translation: Member of the Tribe—in other words, a Jew.) I hated the term, and would refuse to answer. Most of the time, I had no idea what my friends were. To this day it is the last way I categorize someone hating the concept of "us" vs. "them." Besides, if anyone was "other" in my family, it would definitely have been me. In "The Family Crucible," authors Augustus Y. Napier and Carl Whitaker write that families assign specific roles to each person. Mine clearly was "the problem child." The family member everyone could focus on. While my parents probed, pried and invaded all our privacies, I was everyone's problem, to be discussed and dissected. I was deemed "overly emotional," "way too sensitive," "ever the actress." If I became impassioned on a subject, or rejected my brother's teasing, he called me Sarah Heartburn (referring to the great French actress and film star of the late 19th and early 20th centuries, Sarah Bernhardt.) And when he wanted to be truly disparaging, he called me Marjorie—a reference to Marjorie Morningstar, the Herman Wouk character. Like me, she was Jewish, from a middle class family, brought up in a building on Central Park West two streets up from where we had lived. She was also an aspiring actress. While the character in both movie and book started out as a young woman, vivacious, pretty, and with plenty of friends, Chuck intended his barbs to mean a stereotypical Jewish girl not talented enough to have a career in the theater. (I'm quite certain he had never bothered to read the book. The movie would have been more his style.) Actor or artist meant neurotic.

Neurotic meant crazy. Crazy meant in need of a shrink. Which is why I have no doubt it was my brother who came up with the idea I go to one. I didn't fight it. The thought of having someone's ear who would listen, perhaps take me seriously, maybe even convince my parents I wasn't nuts sounded heavenly. One was found—literally down the block from us though not diagonally across like Dr. B would be some six years later.

My appointments were scheduled for Monday evenings at 7. From 6:30, when dinner started until 6:50 when I fled the table to race out of the building and down the street, I endured my father's rants.

"I need to pay $25.00 for her to go complain about us? That's what she does, right? Am I right? Am I? We're paying good money for her to talk about us. *Meshugga!*"

By the time I got to the shrink all I could do was discuss the dinner's conversation. "Could you talk to them?" I begged. "Tell them I'm not crazy?"

The doc agreed and one evening, right after dinner, my parents—camouflaged with sunglasses, hat brims pulled down and coat collars up—slunk into the shrink's office. Whatever was said—and I have no memory of the visit itself—nothing changed. I terminated therapy soon after I told the therapist about a kiss I'd received from a classmate, one I'd found off-putting. "It's because he reminds you of your brother!" the doctor declared. It turned me off therapy for the next few years. Sometimes a slobbery kiss is just a slobbery kiss.

Back at the Playhouse, I spent my days torn between Sandy and Martha. Jane Dudley designated me to lead the girls (as we were then called) across the floor when Martha taught; a man from the company led the boys. I can't imagine who except Sandy could have detained me, but one day I arrived late for class with no time to warm up—everyone poised to move across the floor. Avoiding Martha's eyes, I ran to Gene, her male demonstrator, and in a whisper asked what we were doing. As is the way with dancers, his hands acted out the steps: bending up and down at the wrist for the prance, prance, prance; a twist of the hand for the turn in the air; then palms away, prance, prance backwards. I quickly took my place in the front of the line and took off. Prance, prance, prance, UP! And as I came down, my foot buckled beneath me. The tendons ripping apart could be heard echoing across the room.

"Don't move!" Martha orders as she glides towards me.

Desperate to redeem myself for having wrecked her class, I tell her I'm fine.

"Don't move!" she repeats.

I swear again that I'm fine and she explodes at my insolence, "If you're so fine, get up and show me!"

I stand, lift the injured leg, and as my toe hits the floor, down I go, writhing in pain.

Martha made me attend every dance class for the next three months. On crutches I could do no more than look longingly at the other actors moving in unison. The minute my leg healed, I was at her school on Saturday mornings taking extra classes using whatever allowance I had to pay for them. If things didn't work out on the acting front, I could always be a dancer.

Making certain I wouldn't be late to one of her classes again, I devised the perfect outfit. It consisted of a black leotard and tights over which I threw a thin wool moss green skirt with an elasticized waist. It could easily be removed for dance and pulled back on for regular classes. When Sandy referred to it as a "schmata," I was pleased he took note of me. When my father condemned it, I wore it in spite. There was an evening when a classmate came to the house for dinner. To be fair I had begged her to come. I wanted to show my father I had friends of quality—that not all actors were "dreck" and "whores." She was a former model with perfect features and a figure to match. A daughter of a general, she certainly knew how to impress. I should have expected she would dress up as the whole idea was for her to make a favorable impression. But when Mom begged me to get out of my usual uniform, I refused. "Why? She's a classmate. We go to school together."

My friend arrived in a form-fitting black dress with a low décolletage, a hem that came just above her knees, stockings with perfectly straight seams, and black suede high heeled pumps. From the moment she arrived I could see Dad's eyes light up. She sat down on the small armchair across from him. My mother and sister looked on from the sofa—both women in Molly Parnas black taffeta dresses. I sat, shoes off, legs curled under me, on the loveseat. Suddenly, Dad waved his glass of scotch in my friend's direction.

"That!" he booms. "That is what a young lady is supposed to look like!"

I avert my eyes to the carpet and my empty pair of loafers.

"And her posture! Look how she sits! Why can't you sit like that?"

I want to tell him she's the daughter of a general. Has been made to sit up straight from the time she could walk. But I say nothing, just bite my lip and pray I can hold back the tears.

"And makeup!" he goes on. "She wears real makeup. Not that black shmutz you put around your eyes."

My friend—who would later call Dad "a letch"—simply demurs with a quiet, "Oh, Mr. Krasne, really."

He's on a roll. Continues in the same berating vein even after I get up and run from the room.

"Go! Slam the door," he hollers which I do, locking myself in the bathroom—my hand over my mouth to stifle the sobs. There's a tentative knock on the door.

"Margo, you all right?"

"Go away, Tessie," I manage to say. And her footsteps disappear down the hall. I am sick of feeling worthless; of Sandy's demoralizing critiques; Dad's disapproval; mother's weariness from being in the middle. I reach in the cabinet for my razor and take out the blade.

Suddenly a woman's voice starts to yell. At first I can't catch the words or who it is so I put the blade down, turn out the light and open the door a crack. It's my sister.

"What's wrong with you?" she's screaming. "Don't you know what you have in your daughter? And you! What kind of friend are you just sitting there taking his compliments? I think you better leave!"

I had never heard her raise her voice like that to anyone, never mind our father, but there she is going after him full-throttle. Then I hear movement in the foyer, the hall closet open, a few more words I can't decipher, and after a moment, the front door slam shut. My sister isn't through. ""She was a porcelain doll. A porcelain doll! Your daughter has depth. Can't you see that? Real depth. What the hell is wrong with you?"

I couldn't believe it. My sister actually talking back to our father? Not only talking, but yelling with more emotion then I'd ever heard her display. Yes, my sister acted as a surrogate mother whenever my parents went away, and yes she'd been delegated to inform me about menstruation, explain masturbation, and mediate the various truces between my father and me. But to defend me to such an extent and with such fury? That was beyond extraordinary! She was actually yelling at Dad that I had depth, that I was special. Slowly I put the blade back in the razor and the razor in the cabinet. I washed my face and reapplied my "schmutz." Then I joined them for dinner. Not one word was said as to what had occurred. Not then. Not ever.

At least Sandy and my father differed in their sexuality. Meisner was gay with two wives under his belt. According to student gossip

one committed suicide, the other had a breakdown and was insti-
tutionalized. I'm convinced if he hadn't exited the closet when he
did, I would have been the third with similar results. There were
plenty of others in class longing for Sandy's approval and recognition, but there's no doubt I would have been it. Two incidents, separated by years, tell it all.

Incident one: in our second and last year, one in which only half
the class was invited to attend, Sandy cast me in a Horton Foote
one-act play. My character, similar to Emily's in Our Town, had a
monologue requiring her to speak out to the audience as if address-
ing the dead. At every rehearsal Sandy stood at the back of the
theater and screamed in a voice filled with disgust, "That's fucking
lousy, cut it, just cut the Goddamn line. If she can't say it, drop it!"
Then he'd slam out of the theater. He did this until I was left with
only a short paragraph. The "f" word—not often heard in those
days—along with his voice coming at me, were knives slicing into
my gut. Was my performance stellar? Of course not. But fucking
lousy? No way. Did I cry? Oh God I wanted to, but two things kept
me in check. My father's trick of pressing a thumbnail into another
finger so hard it overrode the emotional pain, and Bill (soon to be
Wayne) Rogers crushing my hand in his and whispering, "Don't
you dare let him see you cry." I loved him for that.

Sandy walked out on our class before school was over and
departed, ironically, to Hollywood. Even weirder, to be pop-singer
Fabian's coach. At a reunion party that summer, one of his teaching
assistants—admittedly drunk—felt empowered to spill the beans.

"He had slashed your monologue, Margo, way before he gave it
to you to learn." It had been Sandy at his destructive best.

Incident two: At least twenty years later, on a crazy impulse, I
stopped by the Playhouse. Sandy was back teaching; his astound-
ing voice now replaced with a fistula after surgery for laryngeal
cancer. His eyes lit up when he saw me—a smile spread across

his face. "Tuna fish!" he croaked. Tuna his nickname for me after learning my father sold canned tuna. For him to remember instantaneously who I was after all he had been through, after all the students he had seen, told me I hadn't been crazy. There had been an attraction. Not sexual on his part, but as is said: put a masochist and a sadist in a crowded room and they will find each other.

Sandy put one more nail in my theater coffin. Before he left, he cast me as a four year old girl in pigtails for what was to be our showcase performance for agents. Sidney Pollack was left to direct it. Needless to say, I wasn't picked up.

Slogging On

I hated having to search for work as an actor. But oddly, what I hated more was the look in every unemployed actor's eyes, one that reflected my own: "See me! Choose me! Discover me! Me me me!" Still, the hope of being discovered, something every unemployed actors walks around with—was not fantasy on my part. While I'd been incurring Sandy's wrath, assiduously studying, taking classes, my cousin Bob—son of my favorite Aunt—had been spotted by Daryll Zanuck at El Morocco, the place to see and be seen. Within days Zanuck cast Bob as the bullfighter opposite Ava Gardner in The Sun Also Rises. As if that was not enough, soon after, as Bob lounged by a pool in Beverly Hills, Norma Shearer, convinced he was a ringer for her dead husband Irving Thalberg, cast him as her husband in A Man of a Thousand Faces. To say I bristled at the injustice of it all doesn't even come close to how I felt. (Yes, this first cousin is Robert J. Evans. He wrote his own book about our family. So, just to set the record straight, we did not have a chauffeur or a convertible. But then memory is so personal, isn't it?)

Miserable as I was, you would think I would have found another profession. But I had committed myself to the theater and I was not about to admit that maybe another career might be more rewarding. So I kept at it, after graduation managing to land the role of the Maid in the musical "The Boy Friend" at the Red Barn Theater in Northport, Long Island. Most days I spent our breaks rehearsing in the studio. One afternoon I decided to go down to the beach where the rest of the cast was hanging out. They teased me about how I never went into the water and took bets as to whether or not I knew how to swim. Fueled by their dare, I dove into the water and swam from Long Island over to what turned out to be Centerport a long distance away. I didn't take into consideration that once there I'd have to swim back. On the return trip, totally out of steam, I clung onto boats in between strokes, unaware my feet were being cut up by barnacles. For the next four performances I had to sing and dance "It's So Much Nicer in Nice" in the air—the chorus boys taking turns holding me up so my feet wouldn't bleed out onto the stage.

Back in New York a classmate from the Playhouse called to say there was an open casting call for Playhouse 90's production of For Whom the Bell Tolls. I had no idea as to why these were called cattle calls until I arrived—every actor in New York had to be there. We were herded into a large room as the director, John Frankenheimer, walked up and down scrutinizing us all. He was known to demand, and get, total control over every element of his productions. In his late twenties, tall, good looking and intense, he had already received enormous acclaim. When he pointed at me to step out of the line, I almost fainted. My God! I had landed a part. A real one! On Live TV no less. (My cousin wouldn't be the only one to be plucked for a Hemingway play.) I ran home ecstatic. I waited anxiously for a script. None came. I was simply to be an extra in the opening scene.

The setting was that of a war-torn village during the Spanish Civil War. I was to stand with other women draped in black widows garb. There was a young girl next to me. In front of us a motorcycle and rider, a stunt man. We all wondered where he could possibly ride it on such a small set. Turns out he was to head towards us and stop just before he got within inches. Frankenheimer appeared, spied a friend of his who had come to watch, told him he should ride the bike. The friend let it be known he'd never even been on one. Frankenheimer was dismissive—told the pro to give his friend directions, then called, "Action!" We heard the bike rev up, watched as it came towards us and tried to scramble out of its way as it crashed into the wall behind bringing the set down on top of us. I threw myself over the little girl, a piece of the set hitting my back, and before I could figure out what had happened, or get up off the floor, CBS execs were handing us release forms that stated we hadn't been harmed in any way. We all signed—the only way we stood a chance of ever working again. With all that, the live production opened with actual newsreel footage of the Spanish Civil War followed by the opening of our scene which paled in comparison.

I managed to land a few episodes on a half-hour live TV courtroom drama The Verdict Is Yours. The audience, consisting of twelve ticket holders, sat as the jury; actual lawyers portrayed the judge and the attorneys. The script presented to us was in outline form. We were to create our own dialogue. I had a few things going for me. I could cry, even sob, on cue. And as for creating my own dialogue, improvisational acting was a mainstay at the Playhouse. I had also spent much of my life imagining scenes filled with love, death, and fame. (My best attempts were the eulogies delivered over my coffin by my father. His were the most heart wrenching, filled with innumerable *mea culpas*. "She was the most beautiful daughter. The most talented. Oh, Lord! Why didn't I tell her I loved her? Oh, please, please forgive me!") In other words, dialogue came easy for me. I was hired, more than once.

Getting Notes

All the while my father kept at me to find another means of support. If I wanted him to pay for singing lessons, then I had to take typing and shorthand. So I went to typing school and learned to type fast, but never accurately. Rather than shorthand, I took up Speedwriting, a far simpler system than Gregg . I never mastered it and thought it rather bizarre I should be practicing my shorthand in between takes on a set where my paycheck was going to be $1000 for a week's work—this in 1959! Of course there were 51 other weeks to contend with when I wasn't employed, but then …

I got called for another live show, The Guiding Light, to play a Shaker woman. I arrived at the set filled with expectations of a real role, but no, I was one of eight women, dressed in drab Shaker dresses who were to dance around in a circle to Simple Gifts, the Shaker hymn. It wasn't a total waste. I met Sue L., another actress.

She had come with the same expectations and we bonded immediately in our disappointment. She lived with her husband a few blocks from my parent's apartment, was definitely anorexic—though the word was not used at the time—and within no time, had me following suit as the camera supposedly put on ten pounds. I was already thin, but began to turn down all my favorite foods until even one grape was too much to put in my mouth. I lost over twenty pounds as well as my period in less than three months. My anorexia came to an end when a painter friend of Sue's asked me to pose for him. The result: an excruciatingly thin me with apple in hand. It was so frightening to look at I slowly learned eat again though the fear of gaining weight would never leave.

Sue and her husband fixed me up with the playwright Ira Levin whose adaption of No Time for Sergeants was a success on Broadway. We had a few dates—none of which I remember. I was so frightened of not being what he wanted I don't think I was mentally present. After the second date both Mom and I skipped over the "getting to know you" phase and in our minds went straight for the altar—the combination of an actress married to a successful playwright tantalizing. At the time I was working part time for the producer Lucille Lortel who invited me to spend Christmas in Florida with her on her houseboat. Idiot me! So afraid of missing Ira's call, I turned down the invite. His call never came. At least not until years later when he saw my name in the NY Times 'Letters to the Editor'. His first question, "Are you the Margo Krasne I knew a long time ago?" I was so surprised he remembered me. He asked me for dinner and when I said yes, told me to be at his apartment at 6:15 sharp—dinner would be at 6:30. My curiosity wouldn't allow me to turn it down. His apartment was a large two bedroom on Park Avenue mostly done in monochromatic colors. Living room and foyer: brown and white; kids' room: navy; and his: red. When I say monochromatic, I mean most everything in each room was of those colors: floors, ceilings, walls, furniture. Dinner was served in the living room on a narrow table against a wall near the entrance—the 6:30 appointed time because the cook wouldn't serve a minute later; our conversation was stilted exactly as it had been years before. I left knowing I hadn't been the only one lacking in social graces.

It wasn't just my father who believed actresses—as opposed to stars—were whores. Lots of producers agreed with him. For instance, David Susskind. Somehow I managed to secure an interview. I was on a high.

I'm seated in his office, my portfolio of head shots next to my chair. He leans back in his chair, tossing his feet onto his desk.

"So!" the little big man says. "You graduated the Playhouse."

"Yes," I say, drawing out the vowel to show off my dulcet tones. "And I've done some TV."

"You ever been in love?"

I find the question strange and try to think of a smart answer.

"Well, have you?" he demands.

"I guess not," I mumble. "I've never been married."

He picks up the phone; calls in his right hand man. "Take her out and break her in. Then bring her back tomorrow."

I pick up my portfolio, get to my feet and walk out his door.

So much for making it big.

Looking for Work after The Playhouse

There were a number of other David Susskind-like scenes, even more in which I was told that due to my height and looks, I wouldn't come into my own until I was older, say in my forties. "You're more of a character actress, kid. You know—an Eve Arden, Eileen Heckart type." But none of these encounters reached the level of the one with Mike Nichols.

A young actor I'd known at BU called with tickets to see the Eileen May and Mike Nichols Broadway show. I donned one of my two "good" dresses—a magenta wool—and was ready to go.

Chivalry still in, he offered to pick me up at the house. The night of our date, a snow storm raged and Mom and I started to battle over what coat I'd wear. I was happy with my cloth; she wanted me to wear her mink. I was not yet aware of animal cruelty—this was 1960—but the idea of walking out in a mink coat horrified me. I was a starving actress after all (forget I was living on Fifth Avenue) and the last thing I wanted was to look like some rich kid trying to break into show biz—or worse, Marjorie Morningstar.

My "date"—a gorgeous young man whom I assume, in retrospect, to be a closeted gay—arrived. Concerned we'd miss the curtain, he begged me to give in and wear the mink so we could get going. I finally did and off we went.

Our tickets were third row center. We were like two kids in a candy store, up close and personal to two hilarious actors. We both had raucous laughs (I still do) and Nichols could not help but take notice of us—though really my date. At the curtain we were on our feet applauding when Nichols motioned for us to come backstage. OMG as they now say. Two wannabe actors invited by a Broadway star backstage. Can you imagine? It was a heady moment only made headier when Nichols invited us to go with him to Sardi's. The waiter led us to a corner banquette and Nichols positioned himself between us. My "date" bubbled up about how wonderful the show was, how we couldn't believe he invited us and how we both hoped someday to land parts on Broadway. I kept pinching myself this was actually happening. Then, out of nowhere, Nichols turned on me.

"You think you're an actress? You nothing but some rich Jewish kid who thinks she can make it in the theater. Bet you can't act at all."

I was stunned. "No, I'm an actress," I mumbled. It was all I could get out.

My friend rose to my defense. "Mr. Nichols, honestly, she's

really very good. Walked off with all the leads at BU as a freshman! Graduated the Playhouse. She's for real."

Nichols kept going at me until his venom was used up. Then he turned away from me and lavished positive attention on my friend. Neither of us knew exactly what to do. I couldn't understand how I, or more likely the damn fur coat, could have provoked such a tirade. Then, a few years ago, I watched a program on Nichols' life. Seems he had been born a rich Jewish doctor's kid in Germany who had to flee the Nazis with his family leaving all behind. A Jewish girl in a mink coat must have represented all that had been lost. (Or perhaps the rumors about Nichols being gay had some validity. He just wanted me gone.)

For years, my high school sculpture The Washer Woman sat in a bookshelf in the den (aka my room.) Whether out of spite that I still had to share the room with my father whenever there was company, or wanting to leave my creative imprint somewhere, I purchased a sculpture stand with my meager earnings, along with Plasticine clay, spread newspaper on the red carpeting, and started sculpting again. (I have no memory of what form the pieces took or if I even finished any.) On Dad's card playing nights I shoved the stand into the closet, and headed to my "back" room. Whether after I moved out I retrieved the stand or bought a new one, I don't remember.

As much as I longed to escape my home, my friend Janey from high school—the one who would hire me to work over Christmas in her shipping room—needed to escape hers. After finishing college, she had taken off for California to be a personal assistant to Anthony Quinn. Whether she got the job through her uncle who was a Broadway lawyer or a college friend whose family was well-connected in Hollywood—one whom I would one day reach out to—I am not certain.

It had been a few years since Janey and I had been close, but suddenly I began receiving phone calls enticing me to join her in LA. As she put it, I could escape my parents' watchful eyes, continue to work on The Verdict is Yours for it too had moved to L.A.—and together we could have a blast. I begged my mother for the airfare, got my brother to teach me to drive—which he did in two weeks' time, passing my drivers' test mainly because I could parallel park and the examiner liked my legs—and was packed and ready to go when I received a call from Janey. She had to leave for Spain with Quinn, but I could take her place in the apartment—her roommate had agreed to stay on. I didn't have the guts to back out, not after selling everyone on the idea. With great trepidation I left New York to find fame and fortune in L.A.

Camp Hollywood

The walkway led up to what went for an apartment building in L.A. in 1961—a white stucco, two story complex, directly behind the Beverly Hills High-School. I was to share the bedroom, but hang my clothes in the hall walk-in closet. Janey's clothes had filled it to the brim; mine took up a quarter of one bar. There was a pull-out sofa and within a few weeks I decided it was more to my liking. A room of my own had always been my preference even if it meant being lonely—that old adage we are more comfortable with what we're used to rather than what we long for.

It took me ages to realize I'd been lured to L.A. under false pretenses. Janey's roommate had never planned to leave. Janey just needed someone to take over her share of the lease while she was in Spain. In Janey's defense I am certain she rationalized her behavior believing she was getting me out from under my parents' prying eyes. Whatever, I was now in LA and someone, perhaps Janey, had arranged a screen test for me at one of the studios. So on day three of my arrival, my roommate lent me her car—an old Olds without power steering—and off I went. It was my first time driving alone and I could barely navigate the twists and turns of Laurel Canyon. By the time I arrived at the studio my hands were glued to the wheel, the blood drained from my body, and I could not speak. Obviously the guard had witnessed this scene before.

"From East are you?" he said.

I nodded.

"First time in the Canyon?"

Another nod.

"Sit tight!"

He made a call; my contacts cancelled the test; and two men ushered me home. One drove my roommate's car with me in it; the other the studio's. They didn't set another date.

I had long wanted to rid myself of my virginity—amazing how much a hymen could weigh in the late 50's early '60's. If I told a man I was still a virgin, chivalry reared its head and he kept a hands-off stance. Others labeled me a professional virgin—a misnomer. Professional virgins grow their hymen back after every deflowering. Mine was still very much intact. Women friends weren't much help either. Some pretended they'd already lost theirs, when they hadn't; and others wanted me to hold out for marriage—something they hadn't bothered to do themselves. After carrying my virginity around all through one year of college, two years at the Playhouse and Summer Stock, I'd had it. Much like a Victorian girl on her wedding night, I decided to pass the petting stage, of which I had rarely if ever partaken, and go from almost never been kissed to let's get it over with ASAP. So when I happened upon a film editor—from somewhere south of the border—dark haired, attractive, with great eyes, and older by twenty years, I decided he was it. I would let him woo me until I fell madly in love and my deflowering could take place. The wooing lasted all of a week.

My neighbor Dot, a nurse, had become my confidante and advisor, and booked me into one of the top gynecologists in L.A. (For some reason I've had a lot of Dots and Dorothys in my life as well as a number of Gails—maybe it's just the era into which each were born.) Anyway, only in L.A. would the gynecologist look like Gregory Peck. He fitted me with a diaphragm making me insert it over and over until I got it right. Then he began his lecture: "The jelly is more important than the device itself. It's what kills the sperm. That's why it's called spermicide. Understand? Do not scrimp. It's your protection. Get it?" I got it.

My soon to be deflowerer and I went out for a dinner, but all I remember of our foreplay is walking into his so-called "home." Whatever fantasies I'd had dissipated upon entry. It was a one-room shack. His excuse for his digs: his Ex had taken him for everything he owned. He poured us wine and put Lucho Gatica on the phonograph. One sip and I headed for the bathroom. It was long and narrow. A single bulb hung overhead. Heeding the doc's words, I slathered on the jelly. The diaphragm leapt from my fingers like a frog escaping capture. No matter how I tried to hold on, each time it flew across the narrow bathroom landing splat in the far corner. On the fifth try, the tube almost empty, Lucho called out to me—I have no memory of my lover's actual name. "Cara, can I help? You okay?" He sounded exactly like Desi Arnez.

A few more attempts and I washed the damn thing off, inserted it dry—squirting whatever was left in the tube in after—and said a prayer I wouldn't get pregnant. Then I made my entrance with one of his used blue and red striped towels wrapped around me. (I would have preferred all white—more of the virginal Doris Day look—but none were available.)

"Ah, Linda, come here," he said holding back the sheet.

I was dying to see what an erection looked like, but had been taught not to stare. Just like I was taught to give up my seat on a bus to anyone older than me, to choose from the right side of the menu at all times no matter who was buying and, at all costs, to remain a good girl. I could hear my dad's "Don't let some *Trombernik* bum wipe his hands on you like a towel." Well, so much for that. This was going to be a bath sized wipe.

Any thought my first time would be fun was quickly dispelled. It was work. Long, hard, painful work. The doctor said he had cut away some of the hymen to help the process along. He should have used a chisel. The next morning I was the perfect cliché staring into the mirror to see if my new found status showed. But only a tired face stared back at me. No change at all. My Latin lover sent flowers and I allowed the romance to continue for a week or so more. Then I ended it. Mission accomplished.

For weeks after, I was consumed with the irrational fear that somehow my father knew I was spoiled goods. I'd be in my rented flimsy Toyota on the freeway—the wheels always seeming to be a few inches off the ground—fully expecting God—that is Dad, to strike me down. I didn't have to wait long. My comeuppance came in the form of a WSWD. Translation: Window Shopping While Driving. Whether I caused the pile up or just added to it, I will never know. I do know it had been hard to resist Saks Fifth Avenue's windows having spent so many years staring at them from New York taxis. It took the police and Fire Department almost four hours to pry me out as I was squashed between what I'd find out was an old Caddie and a crate of a Chevy. I couldn't move; the steering wheel's thin metal rod imbedded in my chin. As the firemen cut sections of the car apart I could feel the blood dripping down my face.

I desperately wanted them to call Dot, but had a rough time communicating between the noise from the Jaws of Life and the rod in my chin. Thankfully I had enough speech training to get out a few sounds that eventually sounded like Crestview—in those days telephone prefixes were names of places not numbers—and using my fingers, I gave the officer, who was trying to keep me calm, her number. Somehow they found her and she contacted one of the best plastic surgeons in town.

I lay on a gurney in an ER—a Resident standing over me ready to stitch. I asked him to hold off. Told him a surgeon was on his way.

"I am a surgeon!" he said, obviously put off.

Then, just as he was about to insert a stitch, in strolled my savior. "I'll take over!" he said to the young man. Then, to me, "Want to watch?"

I nodded and he turned on a screen above. It was fascinating. There was a chin—no longer mine—and his fingers. Being able to watch him work removed me from the process. Yes, I worried he'd discover the cartilage—this years before my confessional—but he never said a word. Just threaded his way through forty stitches.

"A lucky gal, you are," he said and I didn't argue.

The day of the crash I'd been on my way to a photographer. Sadly his name escapes me so I'll call him Ken. We had made an exchange: I would pose for him; he would repay me with shots for my book. I had already filled my end of the bargain before the crash occurred—one of the portraits won him a national prize—but the crash had delayed him fulfilling his end. As I was waiting for the car rental company to decide if they'd loan me another, Ken arranged to come to me—equipment and all. We decided to shoot inside the apartment and outside in front of my building. When we finished he invited me to join he and his wife for dinner even though he'd have to drive me both ways.

Thrilled to get out for an evening, I raced inside to change. I'd tried on a number of outfits for the shoot, so while he piled his equipment into the car, I set about putting away my clothes. I was standing in the walk-in closet when I felt a presence. Did I hear breathing? I don't know. I just turned and there he was. Massive. Tall, blond, crewcut. Who was he? A friend of Ken's? All I could think was it had to be a joke.

"Who are you?" I ask, my breath leaving me.

"I'm going to eat you," he said.

Why was he using my father's favorite phrase?

"Yeah, gonna eat you." He repeats and slams the door shut.

I freeze. Try to scream but nothing comes out. I force myself to grab the door handle, but it won't budge. I'm locked in. I will my arms to hit the door. The movement opens my throat. I scream for Ken and try the handle again. This time the door flies open and I am thrown to the floor. I can see through the living room windows the man run out of the building, and collide with Ken knocking him to the ground. Then he disappears.

Right before Closet Man

There is such a thing as weak in the knees. Mine were water. I found it impossible to stand and crawled on the floor to the phone pulling the cord so it fell off the table. Ken came inside and collapsed onto a chair.

"You okay?" he asked. I could only nod. "Heard the screams. Had no idea it was you."

My fingers were shaking so hard I could not get the dial to turn. Finally I reached an operator. Told her what had occurred. Asked her to send the police. Just as I hung up, a tiny man—no more than 4' 7", wearing a three piece grey suit and toting a brief case— a strange site in L.A.—appeared in my doorway.

"Miss Krasne?" he says as he makes himself at home by sitting, uninvited, on the sofa.

"What do you want?" Ken asks.

"I'm an insurance agent," the little man says and starts pulling out papers. "Miss Krasne had a car accident."

"We know," Ken says. "Look we've just had an incident here. Can you come back another time? We're both shaken up."

"Good!" the little man says clearly pleased with himself. "If she's that upset, she'll tell the truth." Obviously, he was not my insurance guy.

He begins to barrage me with questions and somehow I am able to lie my way through every answer.

"So, Miss Krasne, how fast were you going?"

"Speed limit."

"What were you looking at?

"The road. You know, ahead of me."

"Really?"

"Really."

"And how long have you been driving, Miss Krasne?"

"A while."

He didn't stop until the cops appeared in the door. There were three of them. All young.

"Had a problem here?" one asks.

"There was a man. He locked me in the closet. Said he wanted to eat me."

They nod to Ken. "And you? Who are you?"

"A photographer. Miss Krasne's photographer. We'd just finished a shoot and ..."

They cut him off. "And you?" to the little man.

"Miss Krasne had a car accident. I'm an insurance adjuster."

"Really. And you, Miss Krasne. What do you do?"

Well, even I could tell this was not going to sound great. Ken wasn't my photographer. He was a photographer who happened to be photographing me. But there was nothing I could do but answer,

"I'm an actress," I say, sounding guilty as hell.

"Sure you are. So tell us again what happened."

I wanted to peel the smirks off their faces. It was clear they thought it all a publicity stunt. They made me repeat my story a number of times. Then they left along with Munchkin man. I called my roommate who agreed to come straight home from work. We were locking the windows and doors when the phone rang. It was the landlady. "You had police! You whore! Whore! I want you out my house!" As they say, you can't make this stuff up.

Panicked the attacker would return, frightened of being evicted,

I decided to do the one thing I'd sworn not to do: use connections. (I actually thought I could make it in Hollywood on my own.) I reached out to Janey's friend, the daughter of a prominent Hollywood mogul. She called her dad, who, in turn, contacted the Chief-of-Police. Within hours a top detective arrived with an entourage of what appeared to be rookie cops. He called the landlady and assured her I wasn't a prostitute. Then he had his men question me. "Describe him."

And I did. "Tall, six one, white, blond, crew cut, brown eyes, looks like a college football player, but too old to be one, around two hundred twenty pounds." I was surprised at how much I remembered and how accurate my description would turn out to be.

"And exactly what happened?"

Again, I went through the encounter, step by step. After a while the chief took me into the bedroom, sat me down on the bed. "Listen, you're embarrassing my guys. Leave out that bit about him eating you."

"I don't understand. It's my dad's favorite expression—I mean when he's pinching a baby's cheek."

"Trust me," my new savior said. "It has nothing to do with a baby's cheek, but where they come from."

For the next weeks a group of detectives came by morning and afternoon with mug shots for me to review. Too frightened to leave the house, I spent every day making Duncan Hines cakes—my roommate supplying me with the mixes. I served them up to the cops with coffee. One morning as I went through the latest batch of pictures, my hand started to shake.

"Is that the guy?" one asked.

I didn't respond. I needed to be absolutely sure. I set the picture aside and continued through the stack.

"Damn!" I said when another face sent me shivering. "It could be either one!" I wanted to cry. "Obviously, I don't know anymore."

"Same guy taken a year apart. Relax. We've got him. He's locked up."

It would be the first time in weeks I could go outside. The Chief checked in on me a few times. It made me feel safe and guilty all at once. What about those actresses who had no one to call? What was it like for them?

In the end, I didn't need to testify, because nothing really had happened to me. Not true of another woman as the Chief explained. She'd arrived in court in a wheelchair. One to which she'd be confined for life. He had beaten her to a pulp. "Exactly what he planned to do to you. Reason he locked you in the closet. By the time you threw yourself at the door a number of times, you'd be too exhausted to fight him. If your photographer hadn't been there ... Someone sure must be watching out for you. "

Now freed to move around, a new rental car in my possession, I made an appointment to see Sandy Meisner. What I expected, I don't know, but out of leads, I figured meeting with him couldn't hurt. I sat outside his office waiting; there was another woman in the room. She kept her face hidden behind a newspaper. I peered around assuming it could be someone famous. But no! There she was, my father's living room "paramour." I said hello, she lowered the paper ever so slightly, said, "Hello, Margo" and raised it again. I felt erased. It was clear California wasn't welcoming me in any shape or fashion. I saw Sandy for all of five minutes and remember little except wondering what the hell he was doing sitting behind a desk at a film studio.

One would have thought by this time I would be more than ready to return home. But I wasn't. Whether because it would have been admitting defeat or I really couldn't face what awaited me once there, I do not know. At home all eyes were on my sister.

She had been diagnosed with breast cancer a year before. In one of our rare calls—calling across country was expensive back then— she told me they had found a lump in the other breast. Cancer was still a taboo subject; removing a woman's breasts a last resort. Her two doctors, Pack and Adair—names embedded in my memory— fought with each other for six months whether or not to remove hers. A battle I'm convinced killed her. But she didn't tell me to come home and I didn't ask if she wanted me to. Even with my sister having come to my defense and her role as my surrogate mother, we were not close. I have more images of my sister with my mother than by herself. As often as I accompanied Mom places, as often as she took me to Schrafft's or shopping or doctor appointments, I never believed I could gain the closeness she had with my sister. All this as a way to say I wasn't heading home to New York. Besides, it was only the first week in August. Sleepaway camp usually lasted till the end of that month.

I thought of calling my cousin Bob. His mother, my favorite aunt, had been diagnosed with a terminal illness and I felt the need to reach out. At the same time, I didn't want him to think I was looking for a way through Hollywood's gilded doors. Now, well you may say, if I'd truly wanted to "make it" I would have used whatever means possible, but life is never that simple. Of course it dawned on me that maybe he could be of help. But he was having his own problems. As a matter of fact, my arrival coincided with his well-documented period of being seen as a pariah. He came out of nowhere to land a juicy part in two movies—a clothing sales-man no less—his brother having been the Evans of Evan-Picone. So no, I didn't want his help though if things had been different, I most likely would have. Still, I called and reluctantly—I was after all a kid cousin with whom he'd had little contact—he told me to come over to his hotel. It was the strangest visit ever. The room was dark, uninviting. He was clearly depressed and agitated. He sat the entire time with a piece of plastic—perhaps a dry clean-er's bag—wrapping and unwrapping it as if it were a yarn of wool he was trying to make into a skein. I wouldn't see him again until years later at the funeral of his brother's ex-wife and two children.

I landed another live TV court show, but it took only a day or so to shoot, and with so much time on my hands, I once again turned to sculpting. I found my way to the studio of Pegot Waring, a well-known California based sculptor, and spent the rest of my days in L.A. elbow deep in clay. I don't think I created a single piece—Pegot was intent on my learning to throw the clay until all the air bubbles disappeared and it would be ready for firing. There was always a split second reticence—something that would never leave—before I dug my arms into the barrel; then once my arms were immersed in the wet mud, I would delight in the sensation. I could compare that pause to certain sexual acts—but I'll leave that to the reader's imagination.

The insurance for the accident settled; an obvious dearth of roles; and a longing for a change of season, I went out in front of our building and did a rain dance. Perfection can be boring. Then swearing I would get the hell out of my parents' home for good, I returned to New York at the end of August. I set my moving out date: March 17th St. Pat's Day. It seemed as good a date as any especially as my only real laurels up to then rested on a school production of Finian's Rainbow.

———————————————

As it turned out I was needed back home—to chauffeur my sister to and from doctor appointments. Undergoing rounds of chemo, she was too weak to drive. How awful it had to be for her—someone who everyone said "drove like a man"—that mid-twentieth century "honorific" bestowed grudgingly on a very few. My sister's frustration with my driving was unmistakable. And I? Let's just say driving through Laurel Canyon was a breeze in comparison to those trips with her. I'd get out of the car with every muscle in my body tensed to the point of pain. Why not? My parents had told me if I stopped short, my sister's bones could break, the cancer would enter her blood stream and she'd die. In other words, my lousy driving could kill her. (This before seat belts were mandatory or even installed in most cars.) My folks had it wrong of course. Yes, eventually a bone would break and the cancer would spread, but it had to do with the cancer itself, not my driving. Still not knowing that, after three weeks, the pressure became too much and I told my parents they'd have to find someone else. I would continue to help her with whatever else she needed, just not at the wheel. Which is what I did. I took the train to her home in Westchester to help her shower. She could not raise her arms—her movements limited now her breasts were gone. I'd shampoo her hair and clumps would come off in my hands. She oozed anger. She was angry at the world. At life. At her impending death. The water would fall on us both. I tried to behave as if this was normal. We exchanged few words mainly because I had none.

I got a call to audition for a musical revue in Greenwich Village. The composer: Victor Ziskind—a Leonard Bernstein protégé had already hired three of my classmates from the Playhouse: Bill Esper—today a well-known acting coach; Miranda Jones—whom I've lost track of; and Alex Hasselev who went on to found The Limelighters. Victor would be on piano—our only accompaniment except for Alex's guitar. Victor's show Abe Lincoln in Illinois had played on Broadway—if only for a month. His personality, along with his height, was Napoleonic. Still even with the discrepancy in our heights, he had me snowed. (I'd had a thing for piano players ever since seeing Robert Alda in A Rhapsody in Blue at age nine.) I am certain Victor saw a possible conquest—I got the part.

One of my parents' card-playing friends had moved to an apartment on Fifth Avenue at 8th Street right next to Washington Square Park. That I was performing only a few blocks west didn't matter to my father. Those few blocks made all the difference in the world. He saw the Village as a place of evil. "It's filled with

Beatniks!" he would say with fear and loathing. He had proscribed areas where one could travel. It did not include "iffy" neighborhoods filled with what he perceived as not his kind. Even though he had to go to his business in the Bronx—where a large sign "Krasne Bros." could be seen from far away—he would drive never taking public transportation. He even stayed away from the Grand Concourse where my mother's brother and family lived. Mom (and sometimes I) would subway there, but not Dad. A shame. I have pictures of Uncle Al and my father romping together on the beach. But that was before I was born. Before Dad had climbed the mercantile ladder leaving Mom's family behind.

Exiting the house on days we rehearsed wasn't difficult as they took place when Dad was at work. But come the weekends when we performed was another story entirely. Dad would practically bar the door. If I was to be at the theater by seven, he would start in around four. First complaining to Mom about how ridiculous it was for me to be in some "*shleppish* show." Then coming into my room to talk me out of going. Then back to Mom! And then threatening to not allow me to leave at all. It got so crazy I began to ask friends to come by so he wouldn't lock me in. Why I didn't just get up and go to a friend's or a coffee shop rather than sit at home and endure the craziness is beyond me. Was I by then so cowed? I don't believe so, but somehow I stayed in my room, with two friends, only moving when it was actually time to leave.

After a few weeks, Mom, stressing the Leonard Bernstein/Broadway connection, talked Dad into seeing the show. As luck would have it, once again it snowed on the night they chose. All our audiences had been small, but nothing equaled that evening. The coffee house was absolutely empty except for my parents. Victor, the cast and I discussed whether to perform and decided the show must go on. My parents sat themselves in the rear of the coffee house near the door and as far from the stage as they could get. It was as if we were back at the shrink's office: my father wouldn't remove his coat, hat or dark glasses; Mom followed suit. We performed as best we could to deadly silence. Whatever jokes there were echoed back at us. My folks never applauded. It was worse than a rehearsal. At least then we could talk to each other between scenes. We made it through. After we took our bows, Mom was polite enough to applaud and Dad stood up ready to leave. Victor who had already heard about the lockdowns at my house decided to lecture Dad on my talent and how he should be supporting me not trying to thwart my ambition. I tried to shut Victor up as I watched my father's rage build. A few minutes later my father stormed out; mother and me trailing behind. We managed to find a cab. My folks sat in the back; I on the jump seat. Dad began his rant, "That *pisharka putz*" (no translation needed) "Who did he think he was talking to?"

The cabbie egged Dad on. "No *putz* should talk to a gentleman that way." The two kept at it the entire way home.

Of course, the more Dad forbade Victor to cross our threshold, the more inclined I was to sneak out of the house to meet him. Now in heat, I called a woman I had recently met who'd been looking for a roommate. We set a date and without telling a soul, one night—after my parents left for their card game—I grabbed two blankets, a pillow and a suit case—my wardrobe so miniscule it all fit in—and headed to Morton Street in the West Village and the only ugly building on the block.

All I remember about the interior is the bed on which Victor and I culminated our so-called relationship. It ended after a month. I'd never really loved him, or even wanted him that much, but I needed an excuse to escape my home and I allowed him to sweep me away. Of course, in my father's eyes, I was not only defying convention—in those days "young ladies" only left home to get married—I had condemned myself to the likes of purgatory. Dad never differentiated between those who got paid and those who gave it away for free. I had long passed his towel metaphor, I was now a whore. The only one who had it worse than me was my new room-mate Bobbi. My father found it easier to blame her for my down-fall than his own daughter—or himself.

Bobbi's lease was up in a few months and I found a large one bedroom for us in a new apartment complex called Kips Bay Plaza on the East Side. We moved in with no furniture, some bedding, and Bobbi's large purple silk pillow that one of us would try to get dibs on each morning. For a few weeks it was the only thing on which to sit other than the floor. Bobbi had two friends in the building: two gay guys with a very offbeat apartment. Instead of sofas they'd piled mattresses on top of each other and topped these off with Indian rugs. When possible we'd go up to their apartment—after whatever soiree they had ended—grab two of the mattresses, drag them down in the elevator, and use them as beds, returning them the next day. I bought an oak table and chairs along with a cabinet with drawers. I saved the grand sum of $10 by only buying four of the six chairs as they cost $5.00. (Many years later, on a summer day with Susanne away, when I was convinced I'd forever be mired in despair, I wandered into the flea market on 28th and Sixth Avenue—one which no longer exists replaced with a rental apartment building. There, to my amazement, was the fifth chair. Near tears anyway, I completely fell apart, blubber-ing to the vendor that I had been looking for the last two of the set for years. He said his had been painted black and he had had spent weeks stripping it, so mine were probably from another set. When I told him I'd stripped black paint off mine as well, he gave me his at half price. I never found the sixth.)

At 9AM on a Saturday three weeks after we'd moved in, the phone rang. It was Mom. "Your father and I are coming to see where you live. We will be there at 11." Click!

I hung up and yelled to Bobbi, "They're coming! In two hours!"

We panicked. Bobbi's friends had been out of town for a few days, so we'd been sleeping on the floor. We had one oak table, four chairs—still painted black—a dresser, and Bobbi's pillow. Like a maniac, I ran to Metropolitan Lumber and had them cut a 4' x 8' piece of plywood in half. Bobbi took off for the hardware store to pick up a dozen legs. Somehow we managed to get them screwed on just as the bell rang. I walked as slowly as possible to the door allowing Bobbi time to throw blankets and pillows onto our creations to hide what didn't exist.

Dad didn't even look at me. Mom had her "I hate being put in between the two of you look" and I just held my breath. Dad inspected every corner of the apartment from the kitchen, to the living room and last stop, the bedroom. He didn't say a word. Then he walked over to my so-called bed and sat down. Hard! The good news was it held up. I'm not certain about his coccyx.

Neither Here Nor There

I was still trying to get work as an actress while taking jobs that would let me go on auditions. I had already worked for Jean d'Albret Parfums as a switchboard operator; B.H. Wragge, a couture sportswear firm as assistant to the head of sales—retyping her client lists, erasing my mistakes on sheet after sheet of carbon papers when I wasn't in the showroom presenting Wragge's latest collection; and at this point was at an import/export firm as secretary and all around gofer. I had no idea as to what they imported. I did, however, have a mad crush on a man of mystery who worked for the firm, John Collings. He spoke fluent Chinese and would arrive in New York, spend a few days and fly out again. Sexy in his secretiveness, I worked at seducing him to no avail. The main office was in Washington and I never got a grasp as to what we did other than issue bills of lading. Both he and my boss were highly protective of my supposed virginity. Many years later I met John for dinner. He had aged to such an extent that I almost didn't recognize him. I kept staring hoping to find the man I had once found so compelling.

"I've gotten old," he said.

"No, not at all," I lied. (I often wonder how many lie to me when they swear they took me for ten years younger than I am.) Once again I tried to find out what he actually did. His lips were still sealed in more ways than one. I assumed he worked either for the CIA or a similar organization. I never heard or spoke with him again, but the guilt of not being a better liar stayed with me for a long time.

Minus the typing, I was good at all the jobs; not so at landing an acting gig and not that I tried that hard to do so. I would read Show Biz and if there was an open call, I'd go. I stopped taking acting classes, but I studied jazz and modern dance, usually on Saturdays.

At some point the import/export job ended and I went for an interview at Manhattan Sound, a recording studio. This one would be a step up: Secretary/Assistant to the President of the firm—a full time position with far less flexibility, I wavered as to whether or not I should take it. The offices were dingy—the only color to be found was in the receptionist's bright red hair. The boss however was magnetic. Well over six feet, extremely thin, with chiseled features his demeanor had an edge. I told him I was torn. The position might be too all encompassing and then what would happen to the acting? He leaned his rear on the front of his desk, his long limbs stretched out before him. His response emphatic and compelling,

"It makes no difference to which side you jump, just jump off the fence for God's sake!"

I jumped. Directly into his line of fire.

My first paycheck from Manhattan Sound went immediately to a Carlyle sleep sofa. Bobbi managed to scrape together enough for a bed. We decided to take turns as to who got what depending which one of us was going to be up later than the other. At some point I adopted a stray cat who took an instant dislike to Bobbi. On her nights to use the bedroom, he peed in the bed. No matter how we tried to fake him out, instinctively he knew when it was Bobbi's turn. Who rescued the cat from us, I can't remember.

Bobbi and I had become good friends as well as roommates. Yet it was difficult for me. Bobbi was petite, pretty, almost coquettish. I do not mean that in a derogatory way. It's just that men flocked to her and all too often I found myself entertaining her latest beau while she readied herself for her date. I, on the other hand, was tall, thin, and yes, attractive, but I also gave off an air of not needing anyone. I never understood why a woman was supposed to sit in a car and wait for a man to open the door for her, or not light her own cigarette, or anything else that smacked of feminine wiles. I often felt like one of the characters Eve Arden played on television: the single woman who could more than take care of herself. In reality, that's who I was. Would I have liked a man to be in love with me? Yes, but I suspect that if he fell too hard, I would reject him. I had no experience with men who accepted me for who I was; only with those who wished to change me.

My parents visited my apartment one other time. I had decided to be a grown up and invite the family for dinner. Bobbi was heading home to her folks, so the timing couldn't have been better. Of course, Dad refused to come and only acquiesced after my sister intervened. She arrived in a wheelchair, her cancer having spread. I made certain I had everyone's favorites from the special cheese rolls our cook Anna used to make, to steak tartar, as well as chopped liver and herring. Mostly though, I spent the week before scrubbing the inside of cabinets, washing floors, making certain everything was in its place—worried my father would check for cleanliness. I needn't have bothered. Not only did he not look, he sat with his coat and hat on refusing to eat a bite. We all followed my sister's lead and ignored him. About two hours into the evening I found him in the kitchen sheepishly sneaking food off a tray with his fingers.

When we'd first moved into Kips Bay we discovered the developer had forgotten to insulate the area between the second floor—where we were—and the balustrade over the walkway. When the weather turned cold, icy air would come up through the floor boards. I'd come home from work to find half the tenants from our floor having a communal dinner in the carpeted hallway. Two of those were Joan and Phil Ramone, the recording engineer and at the time co-owner of A&R recording studio. Phil often came home late and as my hours also ran long Joanie would often whip us up eggs—the three of us then settling down for a game of Scrabble. Phil often took me to his studio where I might sit listening to Lena Horne or Connie Francis record. One night Quincy Jones visited with his daughter and I took her to my apartment—she was about nine at the time—to show her how to work with clay. In truth, I had no idea the importance of any of these people—except maybe for Lena Horne whom I learned had a mouth on her that was in sharp contrast to the image she presented to the white world.

There came a time when Phil and Joanie's marriage began to dissolve. They had a standard poodle named Zook—delighting in telling everyone the name spelled backwards was a South African euphemism for a female body part. As the marriage disintegrated, they would each leave their apartment on the pretense of walking their dog only to take him down the hallway to mine so they could vent their frustrations. I eventually had to tell both of them that their dog was going to develop bladder problems if they didn't get him the hell outside. Within a year or so we all moved on, each going in different directions.(A number of years later, required to accompany my family to Puerto Rico over a Thanksgiving weekend, I ventured out of my room at the hotel onto the beach only to come upon Phil, his then wife, and new baby. He ordered me a stiff drink and for the next few days was my touchstone of sanity whenever the family dynamic overwhelmed. Skip ahead many years and after hearing his name mentioned on TV, I gave him a call. Within a few hours, he was down at my loft. It was a strange meeting. Apparently he was expecting a "matinee" and all I wanted was a hug from someone I considered a brother. I asked him about his life and he said he was wrapped up in producing Billy Joel. My own life at that point was so immersed in art, I hadn't followed pop music. I don't ever think he got over the shock of my not knowing who Billy Joel was.

I began to sculpt again. Here too I cannot be certain if the clay was a means of artistic self-expression or if because I couldn't get arrested as an actress, I needed to tell people I was doing something artistic. When Bobbi had to leave New York to take care of her ailing mom, I took on another roommate: a Jewish, British, Orthoptist—someone who worked mostly with children to correct weak eye muscles. Besides being kosher, Gillian was 29 and still a virgin. How she and I survived the year together I will never know. We differed on most everything. She wanted a *mezuzah* outside our door—I refused, not liking sign posts of any kind, including crosses or Jewish stars hung around necks. From the beginning the lease had been in my name, so as it was my apartment. I refused her request, letting her hang one on the bedroom door as it would be hers alone. She chose to put it up, hammering loudly, just as I picked up a long distance call from a young man.

He was someone Mom had arranged I meet—a son of a friend of a friend. He lived in Toronto and while I've racked my brain, all I can come up with is he was "a nice, Jewish boy from a good family" who was dominated by his father. I flew to Toronto twice to see him all the while trying to imagine us married. I couldn't. It had little to do with him. My fantasies of walking down an aisle in a white dress were out of habit rather than desire. He took me up in his sea plane—even letting me take the controls—and showed me around Toronto. I have no idea if I slept with him—though it's most likely I did. (Years later Mom said she'd heard he had committed suicide. Whether he did or not, I'll never know. For a while I worried that my rejection added to his decision. Then again, he did have as many problems with his father as I had with mine.)

I couldn't understand Gillian's need to keep a kosher home. (Besides stars and crosses, I also have problems with adherence to antiquated laws that I believe have no place in modern society.) And she hated when my *trafe* (non-kosher food) was too close to her side of the fridge. What I saw, correctly or not, as her disapproval of the way I lived, inhibited me from calling out to her for help the night I was attacked in our living room. My attacker, unlike L.A. Closet Man, was gorgeous—the strong silent type. We had spent the day at the beach along with the couple who had fixed us up. I wondered how I'd lucked out. He didn't talk much. But the look in his eyes—what should have been my red flag—excited me throughout the day. (Amazing the scripts we can write for ourselves when conversation is limited and we decide to fill in the blanks.) All day I convinced myself he was "the one." Mom would be greatly relieved; even Dad might approve. And it wasn't so crazy that within a few hours I could predict our future. Family lore had it my sister knew she was going to marry my brother-in-law the minute she laid eyes on him. And my brother proposed to his wife after only a few dates. (Supposedly my sister also threw a lamp at my future brother-in-law when he asked if she was a virgin.)

The four of us went for dinner and after, not wanting the evening to end; I invited him up for coffee. I meant coffee. I never could, and still can't, get it through my head why the rules should be different for men and women. Why by inviting him up, I had been, to use the vernacular, 'asking for it.' This is not naiveté on my part, but a disconnect between society's rulebook and my own sense of right and wrong. No matter. We went upstairs and I headed to the kitchen to put up coffee, he following right behind.

He grabbed me. I pulled back. Told him, "no!" He tore at my blouse. I repeated, "No!" He became enraged and dragged me into the living room towards the couch. I was so goddamn confused. Had I led him on? Was this my fault? And how could I scream for Gillian? She'd just say I deserved whatever I got. He threw me down and I remembered my L.A. detective's warning, "If anyone comes after you again, don't resist. Save your life." I lay still, not moving while he pushed up my dress and pulled down my pants. He forced my legs apart and I prepared to be torn to shreds internally. Instead, his penis was almost non-existent. Finished, he pulled himself together, did not say a word and walked out. I stood in the shower for over an hour, my mind a blank. (Eventually I learned he had a condition with a name: Micropenis. The emotional damage it has to have caused is more than imaginable. It did not and does not forgive his actions.)

Gillian's contract was up and she returned to England to marry a Jewish sea captain—yes there was such a person; and Bobbi returned to New York. With no acting jobs, I was still at the recording studio that did not attract musicians. Mostly we recorded voiceovers for commercials, newscasts, and soundtracks for films. I began to sculpt heads. It makes no difference whether my boss offered to sit for me or I asked him to pose, but within no time he was coming to my apartment. I'm sure, like Bill Clinton, he didn't think he was betraying his wife—all he was doing was sitting for his portrait while being serviced by an artist. That the artist wasn't being taken care of was of no import to him—nor obviously, to me. How long this went on escapes me. Nor do I know how many times he sat, how long it took to complete the bust, whether he paid for the casting and brought it home, or I paid and gave it to him. Or, for that matter if he even took it. I know I would wait by the phone for his calls that rarely came, and then be available to him when they did. What other details of this so-called affair, I have blocked out—most likely I wasn't psychically present for much of it. My father, hearing I was making a portrait of my boss, grew jealous. "You did one of him and not me?" Knowing it would be a disaster to do so, I put Dad off.

My lease up, and desperate for a place of my own, I found separate studio apartments for Bobbi and me in a building on 21st Street. I constantly moved furniture around in a vain attempt to make it feel larger. This was not new for me. From seven on, when I was ensconced in my sister's room, Mother would find me trying to push the twin beds and bureau from one wall to another in a vain attempt to make it mine.

Still at the recording studio, a few things occurred that bear mention. 1) I was at my desk when Joanie, our receptionist, ran in to say President Kennedy had been shot and I told her it was a lousy joke; 2) Joanie almost bled out on my bed from an illegal abortion; and 3) I was sent on my first and only sales call.

Like most of the nation, I sobbed as Kennedy was buried, went into shock as Oswald was killed and remained glued to the television as the entire horror unfolded. At my desk at the studio I had to hear the haunting sound of the bugle, with the cracked note, play over and over each time a news tape was copied for distribution to the networks. As for Joanie, I managed to find a doctor who staunched the bleeding and didn't report us to the police. But it was the sales call that would eventually have an enormous impact on my life.

A friend referred me to Marc Brown, a producer of music for commercials making a point of telling me that Marc's office manager, Dorothy, ran the show and I should be extra nice to her. I convinced my boss to let me go on the sales call and called Dorothy to set up a date. Obviously, my friend had told her who I was, because I got an appointment immediately. I was buzzed into the building and when I arrived upstairs—at what turned out to be the apartment where Marc lived, worked and held court—the door was open. I walked in and from where I stood could see into a small office in the back where a woman, I assumed to be Dorothy, was standing at a desk, speaking on the phone. She saw me, waved, motioning for me to wait. I remember those few minutes so clearly. Almost as if caught in a black and white photo. Maybe because my friend had built Dorothy up to me, or maybe because it was my first sales call. But I know she was wearing a black suit, not particularly well-fitted, and no makeup. She was older than me, but not old by any means. Her hair was black though not stylishly cut. You got the feeling she could be truly attractive if she bothered, but looks clearly weren't important to her—her smile hid any imperfections. There was no way I could know then that she was nicknamed "Mother Dorothy" to most every one of Marc's clients. Anyway, I never got to speak with her, because after a few minutes passed, a short, pudgy man, who turned out to be Marc, emerged. I didn't even get a chance to introduce myself when he told me to follow him—he had an errand to run. We cabbed it to Lord & Taylor—which happened to be a few blocks from my recording studio. I pitched the studio's merits all the way. Once in the store Marc asked me to pick out a perfume for a woman friend. Loyal to the core, I chose one of two perfumes created by the firm where I'd worked as a switchboard operator. He asked which one, I chose Casaque. He had the saleswoman wrap it, handed it to me, and left me standing in the aisle in shock. I crawled back to the office, avoiding my boss, called Dorothy and asked what the hell had happened. Her reply, "Enjoy the perfume! That's Marc."

On Monday, March 9th, no sooner had I arrived at work, when I was called into my boss's office. "Pack up and leave!" he said. And I did without even asking what I had done. I gave Joanie a hug—who was then in tears over my departure—and went directly to the hospital where my sister lay dying. I was numb from it all.

My sister was now in and out of comas. I stood leaning on the railing attached to her bed. Her eyes opened. "Why are you here?" she cried. I couldn't believe she knew it was a work day, never-the-less morning. I'd been there almost every day though usually after work. I told her not to worry, my being there had nothing to do with her, only that I'd been fired. I didn't tell her—or anyone else—why.

It took a number of tries for me to get this part of my story onto paper. In one of my many procrastinations—and I am any-thing but a procrastinator usually moving way too fast and think-ing later—I decided to look up my old boss on the internet. There were a number of men with the same name. Something told me to click on one in particular. There he was! Older than the man I'd known. But I recognized the skull. I knew it intimately. I had sculpt it! Within seconds I was engulfed by huge, deep, guttural sobs. I clicked off the site. If I'd noticed it was his obituary, I might have had a moment of solace, but I doubt it. In an attempt to regain control, I called Dorothy. She wanted to know why I was so upset. I couldn't tell her. Shame overwhelmed me.

"Did you murder anyone?" She asked in her usual no-nonsense manner.

"No."

"Well, then get it down and out on paper."

Nowadays one might say I was fired for just cause because I had tattled on my boss. Or I could be praised for whistle blowing. After all, we were steadily losing money continuing to exist because he was skewing the figures. Of course, neither is the whole story. As my mother liked to say: "There are three sides to a story. Yours, mine and the truth."

The truth: We were owned by a Canadian company and every so often the man at the head stopped in at our offices. He and my

boss were extreme opposites. Fred, my boss, was tall with chiseled looks that made it appear it hurt him to smile; the Canadian,
Don, was around 5' 9"—my height—slight in build, boyish. Fred:
intense; Don: warm and friendly. At a certain point Fred and I
were no longer involved. Most likely he ended it; bored with it all.
(Did I cry? Probably; I fell apart at the end of all my affairs no matter their length, intensity, or who had put the kibosh on it.)

When the Canadian invited me for drinks, I went and the
old tattler in me reappeared. Whether I was retaliating for being
ditched by Fred or wanted to be the top man's gal, or both, under
the rationale of doing good, I informed Don that Fred could be
stealing, pocketing the money and reporting it as a loss. As it
turned out, it was all true, but Don was in on it as well.

There is a memory of my sitting in the corner of a bar in a booth
having a drink with Don. It is the next memory that still seems so
unreal. While I can visualize the scene: A hotel room with a man
lying in bed; a girl crouched by the bed; and another man behind
her urging her to climb in. I hesitate to occupy her skin. And yet
who else could it have been but me?

The man in the bed was the Canadian. The man standing
directly behind me I had considered a friend. He and his wife—a
childless older couple—had been confidantes, advisors, often having me to their home for dinner. Yet it was he who brought me
to the room and offered me up to Don. Did he do so because he
wanted to make points with his boss? Was he worried about losing his job? Or had I told him of the attraction? I have no answers.
All I remember is crouching by a bed in hotel suite and my once
fatherly friend departing. I do not remember crawling under the
sheets—or having sex, but it had to have occurred. I don't even
remember leaving the room; though it's unlikely I stayed until
morning.

A few months after I was fired, the studio closed. I learned from

Joanie that the Canadian went to jail either for money laundering or tax fraud. I don't know if my boss did, but I think so as there's a gap in the resume part of his obit. I wish the story ended there. It didn't. A few years later the phone rang and it was the Canadian. Swore he was desperate to see me. I told him no, but he begged. Explained he'd been locked up or he would have called. I weakened. This time it was he who crawled into my bed. While having sex, he turned me over and pushed himself into my rectum. I had not heard of anal sex and went into shock. He apologized saying it was how he'd had sex in jail. I felt violated; told him to get the hell out. This being the sixties, Aids hadn't reared its ugly head. Once again, I was incredibly lucky.

The crying has stopped. The crouching girl a distant memory. I can look at the photograph of the bust I did of my boss without feeling the slightest pang. The picture and his obituary on the internet?—I never wish to see them again.

My sister died the day after I was fired. The night before her funeral her husband, my brother and I went into the room that held her coffin and without telling my parents opened it. She was in her electric blue brocade satin cocktail two piece outfit, one she had loved. Her makeup was exactly as she had worn it, her lipstick applied outside the line of her lips—1940's movie fashion. A wax figure thankfully reduced in size from the bloated one that had lain in the hospital bed.

"What a dish!" My brother-in-law exclaimed.

I was taken aback. What I'd expected I'm not sure. A deep wrenching good-bye? Words that would move me to feel something for I was strangely empty. We had been preparing for years for the day she would go, it was only my father who wished her to remain no matter her condition. I could not understand prolonging the agony. But then, as I have already said, I hate suspense. If something is heading my way, I want it over with as quickly as possible.

Perhaps if she had lived, we would have found more in common. Activities other than the Sunday Times crossword puzzle which she was teaching me to master. It was our point of contact. I know at some point in the months before she went to the hospital for the last time, I had sat on her bed and we had talked, but I know that only because, her closest friend and ally, my brother-in-law's sister, commented she was glad we had. What we said remains a blank. What do you say to a sister who is dying when you have your own life ahead of you? Someone who became enraged when I jokingly told her daughter not to marry before I did? (Had she known I never would?) Someone whom I turned to in need constantly, but who never turned to me? Who had yelled at our father that I had depth? Who when I once told her I loved her, left the room as if I had taken a lit match to her shoe, telling me not to be so dramatic?

No, what gnawed around my edges obliterating all other feelings was guilt. Not that I wished my sister gone. But while she had been my mother's surrogate when Mom was away, she was also Mom's other self when at home. I couldn't wipe away the thought that now there would be room for me. I would be needed.

If my father could have shrouded us in sack cloth, tied us to chairs wailing in misery, it would not have been enough. He needed everyone to mourn non-stop. A smile or the smallest laugh was forbidden. For a man who went to temple only on the High Holidays, he now wanted a *Minyan* (the minimum of ten men needed to come together in order to pray in the Jewish faith) at the house morning and night so he could pray for a full week of Shiva. I was not to go home to my apartment. My job: to scrub my parents' bathroom floors—Tessie didn't arrive until 9—help serve the coffee and Danish to the men, and assist with the preparation of food for the guests in the evening. It was alright for my brother to leave, along with my brother-in-law, but not me. As they say, be careful what you wish for.

On the third night of Shiva, desperate for a break, I told Dad I needed some air and went for a walk with my brother's sister-in-law and her husband. We stopped at the Carlyle for a drink. It was the first time I felt human in days. Upon my return, my father smelled the alcohol on my breath and erupted. "You think this is a time to party? Your sister is dead and you go to a bar?" My mother tried to calm him; I had no doubt she would have liked to come with us.

Shiva over, my parents, my sister's husband, as well as my brother and his wife went south to the Doral in Miami. I stayed at my sister's house. I was to look after her kids and answer all the family's condolence notes—three shoe boxes full. I found it reasonable to answer my parents' notes, but my brother's and brother-in-law's as well? Still, I accepted the role pushing away feelings of hurt and anger, but then I had wanted to be needed, so how could I refuse? Besides the condolence notes, I was also to sort through my sister's belongings. To box up what was to be given away, saved for my niece and nephew, or sold—such as the black seal coat my sister had bought even though she knew she might never get a chance to wear it. "Why should his next wife get one?" she'd asked.

As I went about my duties I was not oblivious to the fact I might be erasing what there was of my own life. But then, what was there? I didn't have a job, had no way of knowing how I would pay my rent. What if I actually did take my sister's place? Family friends had suggested my sister's husband and I pair up—keep it all in the family. So, while he and my parents were away, I slept in my sister's bed, pinned up my niece's skirts the way my mother had mine and dealt with my nephew's idiosyncratic eating: only bacon, dry rye bread and well-done hamburgers.

It was in my sister's attic where I found myself. In a scrapbook she had put together—on me. There were reviews from school plays, from summer stock, TV, wherever my name had appeared, she'd cut it out and pasted it in. I leafed through in amazement. Why hadn't she showed it to me? Or at least told me? Still tears never came. It would be months until one day I reached for the phone on a Sunday morning to call her, the crossword opened, that I realized she was gone. But even then, all that came was one enormous sob.

Right before Mom had left for the Doral she had taken me to lunch at the neighborhood coffee shop. "We're redoing our will," she said. "What do you want?"

I reassured her she wasn't dying. Said I didn't want a thing. But she didn't quit. Not through the burger, the French fries, or the coke. She kept eating while my appetite disappeared. The apple pie we always shared sat between us, and desperate for the conversation to end, I gave in.

"I want the piano!"

"Chuck already said he wanted it. I promised it to him."

I finished every last bite of the pie and whatever else was left on the table.

Much of what I did until January of '65 is a blur. I know there was a brief affair with someone who was affianced to someone else. I assume I half-heartedly continued to look for work as an actress, collected unemployment, and spent an extraordinary amount of time with my parents. (My father would mourn my sister for the rest of his life. He made my brother cancel his 40th Birthday party—three months almost to the day of my sister's passing.)

My high school friend Janey's mother had died a year before. During her *Shiva* Janey received a call from a visiting Spaniard. Much to my surprise—I was with her at the time—she invited him over and within weeks they were engaged and a few weeks later she was off to Spain for a test run. The wedding set, she appointed me her Maid of Honor. There were others she was equally if not closer to, but, again, as I was unemployed, I would have the time to take over all the duties her mother would have handled. I felt much like I did when my old roommate Bobbi had a date. Once again I stepped into the role of the single woman, side kick, and all around take-care-of-everyone-else character. The night before the wedding, in a moment of good girl vs. bad girl angst, I sat in bed, pen and paper in hand, and made a list of all the men I had slept with. By then I was twenty-seven and had gotten up to the same number of men when Janey called.

"You sound out of it. What's going on?" she asked.

"I've slept with 27 men—in six years!"

The soon to be bride proceeded to go holier-than-thou on me. "You are going to have to watch it, Margo. You certainly have been way too free with your body."

I ordered her to begin her own count. When she got to my number, I reminded her of one she'd forgotten.

"But that was a one night stand!" she said.

"And what the hell do you think most of mine were?" I slammed back.

We called it a draw.

More and more I hated going on go-sees and auditions; despised the lack of control I had over my life. I was either too tall, not blonde, too thin, too young—come back when you're 40, kid— or whatever reason was given for me not getting a part, forget an agent. I began to search for what my Dad, and others, considered a real job. Two appeared—both for that of a production assistant. One was at a studio that made commercials; the other at an ad agency. Why I even considered the first amazes me as the owner not only held the interview in his apartment, but in the midst of our conversation, suddenly left the room, returning a few minutes later to say he'd prepared a bubble bath for my pleasure. While I declined the bath, I was still not sure which to accept. I called the friend who had introduced me to Marc from a phone booth on the corner of 42nd and 5th for guidance. His answer unequivocal: The agency!

In season one of Mad Men it was referred to as the "Jewish Agency." For those of us who were there it was Doyle Dane Bernbach and on February 1st 1965 it was where I reported to work. I walked into what was to be my office, a drab cell of a room with one metal desk and two chairs. Another woman, around my age, named Roberta was leaning against the desk. We spent the morning trying to figure out if there had been a mistake and they had double hired. It certainly appeared so. Our job descriptions were exactly the same. (We later learned she'd been hired because of her extensive knowledge of film; I because the boss liked my legs.) Our boss, the head of the department, was a replica of my dad, of Sanford Meisner, of ex-boss Fred: seductive, provocative, withholding, unavailable—a tease. Red flags should have gone up and maybe they did. Perhaps why I had called to ask which job I should take. One man wanted to put me in a bubble bath; the other in his bed. I would land in the latter.

I was assigned to a producer and one of the first places he took me to was Marc Brown's. Turned out not only was Marc notorious for his music tracks, but also for his free steak lunches. Dorothy remembered me. Supposedly so did Marc, though with him one could never be certain. Lying was part of his M.O. Coincidentally both Dorothy and Marc's ages corresponded directly to my siblings. Both grew up on the West Side. Dorothy remembered her mom pointing out "There's Mrs. Krasne with the new baby." They would be my new family. As I mentioned, where Dorothy was concerned appearances were secondary—if not tertiary in her book— reading and music far more important, in that order. Divorced, with three children to bring up and no alimony, she rode her bike through the streets of Manhattan, and would do so until well into her 80's. She shopped at flea markets, had little or no visual sense, and was an extraordinary grammarian. As of this writing-at 93, with her short term memory spotty and having taken to her bed,— she still is correcting any slip I make.

Marc, on the other hand, stood in for everything I wished my brother to be: caring, concerned, giving. He took me to the hospital in the middle of the night when I dropped a bronze sculpture on my foot; treated me to an airline ticket to Spain; and flattered my ego by having me write lyrics for a jingle he was working on. When, after a few months at the agency, my new boss openly came on to me and I felt the magnetic pull into a destructive affair, I raced to Dorothy—all of 9 blocks. She handed me the name and number of her shrink, Dr. B on whose couch I reclined on within days. Seeing a therapist no longer had a stigma attached. Almost everyone at the agency went. It was a fad much like the hula hoop and double martini lunches. Most sentences started with, "Well, my therapist says ..."

On my pittance of a salary, Dr. B suggested I ask my parents for help—as long as they didn't pay her bill directly. After much pleading, with Mom as the intermediary, he agreed to cover my rent. Of course I felt guilt. Not easy to bitch about your folks knowing they're paying directly or indirectly. Nor did it help that I could see Dad watching me from his window as I headed up the block. (In 1966 Madison and Fifth Avenues became one-way streets which meant as I walked from the bus to Dr. B's, Dad could see me from his side window—and I could see him peeking out from behind the curtain.) Dad would wait the full fifty minutes to see if I would run up and give him a kiss before I returned to work. When I didn't, even if I pleaded time constraints, he pouted. (Keep in mind there were no cell phones, therefore apologies had to be made once I returned to the office. By then he'd worked himself into a full-blown sulk.)

Dr. B's bent was Freudian. Her view: I'd been repeating the family triangle scenario. My lovers were my father; Mom, their wives, and me? Well according to Dr. B, I was trying to get the "big man" all for myself. I mentally accepted her theory although it never emotionally connected. Perhaps if she'd replaced Mom with my sister it might have made more sense. In retrospect, I believe I was doing the exact opposite from what Dr. B hypothesized. As long as there was a woman, i.e., mother to protect me, I wouldn't be swallowed up whole and destroyed by my lover—not that she had been my protector the day Dad had wanted me to climb into bed, but that was an anomaly. Of course, Dr. B.'s making me see that each of the men I'd picked had qualities akin to my father's put the kibosh on the culmination of the sexual act with them, or at least any enjoyment of it. Destruction was one thing; incest something else. Good sex came with men I didn't care about or wasn't attracted to. Not caring what they thought of me, I could give myself over to the pleasure of it all. Besides, if I didn't love them, I remained in control.

My boss kept plying me with longing looks and sexual innuendos. For the most part I kept the handcuffs on, but the pull was fierce. I managed to keep him at bay until he got the bright idea for me to bring a costume over to where he was shooting a commercial in London. By rights another production assistant was supposed to go. Should have gone. But Jay was Orthodox and highly observant. So our boss switched the flight from Thursday to Friday making it impossible for Jay to travel. Did I beg my boss not to do this? Yes. Did I go with him when he went ahead with his plan anyway? Yes. Was Jay upset with me once he figured out what had happened? Absolutely! And did I feel remorse when a few years later Jay was stricken with a fatal melanoma without ever seeing London? 100%. But it doesn't change the fact I went and spent a great weekend. I poured tea at the Dorchester, bought Wedgewood dishes, and stood outside the Tower of London at one o'clock in the morning with my new lover—who I really didn't want.

One late afternoon in November, New York was hit with a blackout. I happened to be at Marc's for a meeting when it occurred— as was Herschel Bernardi the actor. We all decided to stay put as there was no safe way to get home. During the course of the evening—actually night—bathed in candle light, slightly inebriated— we'd been eating and drinking whatever was left in the kitchen— Herschel and I began to sing duets. Fiddler on the Roof had been running for about a year, and Hesch, as he was known, was going to replace Zero Mostel as Tevye. I knew all the songs and played daughter to Hesch's Tevye using all my powers of emotional persuasion. Without my needing to say a word, Hesch decided I should audition for the role of the oldest daughter. Incredibly, I convinced myself that I could do the show at night and somehow keep my day job, I jumped at the chance.

My fantasy of finally making it to the Broadway stage dissipated when the call for the audition came. It was for the roadshow. I spent hours on Dr. B's couch wrestling with what I should do. If I auditioned and got the part, it would mean leaving her, my job at the agency, and any hope of licking the married man attraction which is what sent me to her in the first place. Worse, when the tour came to an end, I would be back to where I started: no income, no job, no life. I put my Broadway dreams away. It would be years before I could go to a show without pangs of what might have been marring any enjoyment of what was on the stage before me. As to whether or not I would have landed the role, I have no idea. By that time my airways were filled with two to three packs of cigarettes a day. Eventually it would be four.

At DDB-Cigarette in Hand

A few years ago, on a visit from her home in England, Robbie—
my first day office sharing mate—and I spent an afternoon remi-
niscing. We had not seen each other in forty years. She "confessed"
she used to watch me strut the halls and think she could never
compete with "That!" as she put it. I listened in amazement—my
memory of those days so different. She was the top producer's right
hand and confident; she had a steady man in her life; she knew who
she was. Hell, I had wanted to be her.

As I couldn't compete with Robbie and Jay, the two film mavens
in the department, I begged, pleaded and cajoled my way into taking on producing all the radio commercials for the agency. It was
assumed I'd fail, but as no one else wanted the job, my boss gave it
to me. One of the first scripts to cross my desk had the direction: It
is a quiet smoke-filled room. For radio? We couldn't give the writer
the smoke he requested, but we added a few clinking glasses and
lounge piano music to create the desired effect. The poor scripts
kept coming, making it clear radio was low on the agency's totem
pole. Assignments went to first year writers, almost none who
understood radio or were masters of dialogue. I'd heard Bill Bernbach had an open door policy. What no one explained was it didn't
apply to producers—only copywriters and art directors. New to the
world of advertising, I had no idea of the impact he'd had on the
ad world. To me, he was just another businessman who could have
played cards with my Dad—one whom Dad might have probably
made some derogatory remark about when the evening was over.
"His cigars stink!" "He cheats!" "He doesn't shut up!"

At Bernbach's office door I introduced myself, explained the
radio spots were not up to his standards and watched his eyes flash
fury. I was quickly dispensed with and sat in my office waiting for
the dreaded pink slip. Instead, within a short period of time I got
a call from Bob Gage, the head Art Director, who told me to put
together a reel of the agency's radio spots. I did so hand-splicing
them and waited. One hour passed, another, then in walked Bern-

bach, Gage and Leon Meadows, the head writer. Gage nodded for me to hit "play." Other than that one motion, no one acknowledged my presence or asked who had done what. They listened, and as if on cue, got up and walked out. An hour later Gage called.

"What's your solution?"

I told him more senior writers, but more importantly, creative teams. "They're used to working together; maybe it would elevate radio in their eyes." Gage had me attend a meeting of the creatives to pitch my ideas. From then on I worked either with a team or a writer who "got" radio. We began to win awards, and I was allowed to build a department. I was also allowed to add creative input. Of course, not all my suggestions were successful. Such as when American Airlines decided they should have an announcer read their departure times per city as well as their menus on the air. I couldn't imagine anything more deadly. Neither could the writer. I pitched the idea of having an actual flight attendant (in those days stewardesses) be the announcer, and have her recite the schedules using an incredibly sexy voice, making every "10:54 AM" and every "peas and carrots" sound like a Mae West invitation for sex. Everyone, including American Airlines, signed off on the idea. The spots hit the air and played for all of one weekend. It took one woman to call American Airlines screaming she would never let her husband fly with those "expletive" women, for the spots to be pulled.

Part of my job description—a term not used back then—was to direct the actors in the commercials. I spoke their language, felt a connection, but more importantly, I was now in control. (Perhaps it was my new sense of power with which I strode the halls that gave rise to Robbie's "That!") As a producer, I was also responsible for hiring the music houses that provided scores for our commercials. I certainly used Marc—though never exclusively. He was a megalomaniac, destructive to his son, manipulative, but as I said, he was always there for me as I was for him. I brought him business; he brought me an array of incredible musicians from Clark Terry, Tommy Newsome, Bobby Rosengarten, J.J. Johnson, Bucky Pizzarelli to the Fifth Dimension and the Swingle Singers. It was a heady time.

The agency was filled with and serviced by people who aspired to other heights: copywriters who wanted to be published authors; producers who had worked in film and television, but now needed steady employment. There was Mike Stoller, of Lieber/Stoller fame, who, to my shame, I thought of as a jingle writer and went head to head with over the copyright of a particular piece of music. There were those who kept their talents to themselves such as Russ Hoban who would write Ridley Walker for which he gained world-wide attention; those who did it solely for the money; and others who simply loved advertising with all its madness—their kudos gained for writing famed Volkswagen, Clairol, Polaroid ads. In contrast to today where media is consumed on a personal basis, commercials were a focus of those standing around water coolers as much as an episode of M*A*S*H. Everyone saw the same show at the same time. No fast forwards. No plethora of channels.

We also worked pro bono on social issues. All of it bred a sense of importance—at least for the writers and art directors. As I needed to be seen as a creative person as well—not simply a "producer." I made certain everyone knew I was a sculptor. Even got written up in the agency paper with a picture of one of my latest efforts: a mother, father and child—a girl naturally.

The Family

My father had never let up on wanting me to do his portrait. I continued to stall. Finally, worn down, I agreed and Dad arrived, best suit and tie, shoulders back, stern faced as if to say—show me! I captured him in the first sitting. He took one look, swore the nose was too long and ordered me to fix it. I said he couldn't judge a piece before it was finished. He went home and complained to my mother.

"What would be the harm to change it?" she asked.

On the second sitting as he watched me work, Dad became even more enraged. "How could you do this to me? I don't look like that!"

I tried to explain I sculpted what I saw.

He stood up, snapped off the nose, and left.

Marc also requested a portrait of his son, Craig. One I was more than willing to do. The boy arrived late. (I have never understood why one person's time is more valuable than another's.) He was sullen, tired and flung himself into a chair. I'd heard he was a troubled kid, and it showed. I wondered how I could render a portrait of someone who wouldn't sit still for a second. I tried to make conversation, but all I got back were grunts. When I left the room to get some water, I came back to find one of my tools broken. I confronted him.

"Had to happen before I came," he lied—a chip off his father's block. Clearly this was far more than teenage angst. Again I began to sculpt what I saw before me. "I hate it," he said.

"Sitting?" I ask. "Or the piece itself?"

"The piece. It stinks. I don't look like that."

"But you do. At least that's what you've shown me. I can only recreate what I see. My fingers won't lie."

Within seconds he became another person. He smiled, sat back down and posed. "I'll be different if you fix that!" he said, pointing to the piece as if it were a pile of turd. He even apologized for the broken tool. I redid the sculpture. I didn't capture his essence, but his psyche, unlike my Dad's, was far more important to me than any piece of art.

Craig

I learned some years later that Craig had been shot somewhere down south and had to be confined to an iron lung. A few years after that, over one long weekend—one of the weirdest I have ever spent—I was overwhelmed with an insane impulse to call Marc; insane because he had already died of heart failure. I tried to shake the feeling, but the more I tried, the stronger it became—a vise that kept me in its grip for days. Suddenly, what can only be described as "a spell" lifted. Two months later I learned that during my "lost" weekend, Craig had passed away. To say I was unnerved would be putting it mildly. I hoped never to experience anything like it again. I wasn't so lucky.

The second spell-like experience began with the making of a United Negro College Fund radio spot. Most agencies did pro bono ads, and we were either assigned or opted for the Fund. In the process I met Harriet Pitt, the Fund's PR person and Dr. Stephen Wright that year's Fund's president. We became socially friendly and I invited Harriet, Dr. Wright and others over to the apartment for drinks. Dr. Wright was eloquent, learned and kind. My sculptures, visible in the small apartment, attracted his attention. Harriet mentioned they needed an award to be given to LBJ at a fund raising dinner for UNCF and they offered me the job. I was thrilled and created an all too literal piece of sculpture: an upright fist holding a broken chain.

UNCF Award to LBJ

Invited to the dinner in DC, I became obsessed with what to wear as if I were to be the main attraction. Having no sense of what people wore to these affairs, or even the slightest realization the evening was not about me, I found the most outlandish evening dress with feathers around the hem. I remember coming down from my hotel room to see all these people in normal cocktail and business attire. I desperately wanted to run and hide, but Harriet spied me, called me over and I was stuck. My discomfort grew as the evening wore on, as well as my disappointment that LBJ didn't show. I returned to my room, hysterically crying over the phone to Dr. B., the shame unbearable. I never wanted to show my face anywhere again. It took her hours to talk me down. While I wanted to die; I was equally aware I would not act on my feelings.

Skip ahead to January 1973. Harriet and I hadn't been in touch for years; my memory is we didn't part well, definitely something I did which I've managed to block out. Be that as it may, once again I experienced an intense sensation of someone telling me to pick up the phone and dial, only this time I was to call Harriet. For days the more I fought the urge, the stronger it became. Finally I gave up—at least Harriet was alive—and dialed. Just as Harriet picked up, there was a news flash on the TV I had on in the background: President Johnson had died. Both connections—to Craig and Harriet—once again shook me to my core. I never had another one of these so-called spells until after Mom died and I knew she was with me. After she left for Chuck they never occurred again.

Sex ran rampant at the agency. It took over the halls and offices. One of the secretaries even went around giving blow jobs at lunch. The sexual revolution was upon us and I partook along with everyone else. I had been put on the pill by my sister's oncologist as a way to alleviate some of my menstrual cramps. It certainly allowed for spontaneity. There was the day when I walked into a restau-

rant where six men from the agency were eating and I realized I'd
slept with them all. Granted it took me a few minutes to recover,
but by the time I got to Dr. B, I relayed the moment almost as if I
was Margo the Conqueror. "I couldn't believe it, but I'd had each
of them."

"And they all had you," she said, slowing me down for some
time to come.

There would be one more married man in my life; one who
would occupy me emotionally for all too long. I'll call him "L."
He was a composer, piano player, Oscar winner, and a close friend
of Dorothy's. I'd heard about him for years. How they'd known
each other since childhood, how he'd been married, then divorced,
then married again, and was now on his third wife—a woman half
his age. The first time we met was at one of Marc's lunches. From
across the room we bantered about theater, music, politics. I felt
special. Dorothy's great man found me intriguing. Exciting fare.

A few months later, only a few days before my 29th birthday,
Dorothy brought "L" to a session I was running. He was in New
York to work on a Broadway show—his wife of only a few months
preferring to remain on the West Coast. He took us to dinner at
the Russian Tea Room. The same electricity I had experienced at
Marc's ignited again. It was obvious there would be no stopping us.
Dorothy, none too happy, excused herself and went home. Thus
began our whirlwind affair. I set new rules. I would see him only
as long as his wife did not set foot in New York, and under no cir-
cumstances would I play the other woman hiding out from prying
eyes. That I was the other woman, I ignored. We went to shows
in and out of town—best seats in the house. We took a helicopter
back from DC where he had wanted to show me a Civil War bat-
tlefield. We dined out at the best restaurants; we ate in, going over
the latest lyrics to his show. I was his muse; he the great man who
relied solely on me. Sexually we we're duds. Partly because he was
more a romping teddy bear than a sensual lion. Partly because I

had to keep part of me in check. If I allowed love and sex to combine, I would have been swallowed up.

Not that we didn't try to make the bed work. "L" even bought an 8 mm projector and a porno film that he hoped would turn me on. The film strip kept breaking. I tried hard to focus, but watching "L" jump out of bed to constantly try to reset the film in the sprockets, had me cracking up.

At the same time Dr. B tried to wean me off from calling my parents daily. Whether my sister had been the one to set the bar—my brother following suit—now with her gone, it was almost impossible for either of us not to do so. Did I resent the calls? Absolutely. From the Playhouse days on, I longed to be free of what I considered to be a chain around my neck. Yet, not to call produced so much upheaval I found it simpler just to check in. "L", watching how resentful I'd become until the call was placed, took up Dr. B's cry. "Just don't do it. Life won't end!"

I decided to give it a go over a weekend that "L" and I were to spend together. The same fear I'd experience years later at Susanne's thinking my father was overhead ready to swoop down for the kill, went on all day. Still I did not call. By Sunday the fear abated and by Monday—I'd decided to take the day off as long as he was in town—I had forgotten my parents existed. That is until my assistant, who knew how to reach me at the apartment "L" had rented, called.

"They're threatening to send the police to find you if I don't tell them where you are. I've been stalling, but I think they'll do it."

Of course, I called. Even went on the offensive berating mother for involving my assistant in my private life. But in the end it was simpler to go back to the daily calls. Not initially. It took a few weeks until mother's voice softened as it was better for her to have one daughter than none.

When in May "L's" wife came to town, I called it quits. No matter how many letters and calls he tried plying me with, it was over. At least until the opening night of his play which he begged me to attend. "I've told her all about you. That like Dorothy you are one of my New York friends, if you don't come she'll know we were lovers. You have to come. Please!"

I succumbed. Not only did I go to the show, but to the dinner after at Sardi's. We sat opposite each other, "L's" wife and her parents to his side, Linc Diamont, a mutual friend, next to me, and Dorothy beside him. "L" insisted on handing me every congratulatory telegram as if his wife wasn't there.

"Better get a food taster or you won't be alive after dinner," Linc whispered.

I kicked "L" under the table motioning with my eyes to hand one to his wife. He ignored my gestures. He was having a ball.

The show closed six months later and "L" came to New York alone wanting to see me. I fled the city for the Hampton's, panicked I'd be sucked back in. I needn't have run away, because although I found others to bed, I remained emotionally committed to "L" for years. He had been the only man in my life who had ever whisked me away, wined and dined me on a whim, and if he found fault with me, never let it show. (That he had dozens of other muses, some simultaneously to me, I would not learn until years later. Incredibly, some were also close friends of Dorothy. When I asked her why she hadn't told me as I might have freed myself from him way earlier, her only response, "Couldn't." No matter how I pressed, all I got was a shoulder shrug. The only conclusion I can come to was that she could not risk the loss of his friendship, whereas if she kept mum, she knew she'd keep mine.)

Doubts Creep In

It wasn't as if I haunted art galleries or museums—putting myself in the competitive arena way too threatening—Dad's "genius" theorem now totally internalized. But I could also not get away from what I saw, or didn't see, in my work. It would take me months of sessions until I confessed to Dr. B that my work didn't look "professional." Something was lacking. Yes, the pieces were emotional, but what was missing I couldn't articulate.

Gently she suggested I start to study other artists' work—told me to get a book on Kathe Kollwitz, "I believe you will find you have an affinity with her," she said. I left Dr. B's office, skipped my father's mandatory kiss on the cheek and headed to a bookstore buying whatever books there were on this German artist whose work was vilified by the Nazis and who died in 1945.

Her work spoke to me. It was powerful, emotional and figurative. But it also threatened. I read her bio in search of any shred of similarity to my own life, clutching at the most miniscule detail to reassure me I too was an artist. It would be how I'd approach every artist's work I came in contact with—the life first; the art second. I knew it wasn't rational, but my doubts about my own talents were formidable. Still, God forbid I should take a class, or find a teacher. When Dr. B went one step further and gently counseled I study, I slid down into the depths. Her suggestion proved she was simply another person in my life who thought I wasn't special, not truly talented or, God Forbid, simply ordinary. Somehow she convinced me that it was not what she believed and pulled me out of the skids enough for me to find a mentor.

I learned about Bruno Lucchessi, a teacher at the New School, through the man who cast my pieces. I convinced myself that my job at the agency—with hours that went way into the night—would prevent me from taking his regular classes. In truth, I did not want to be one of a group. So on a Saturday morning, with photographs of my work under my arm, I headed to his studio on St. Marks Place. I knocked on his door and he welcomed me in. The studio was small, long and narrow. It had a few sculpture stands, a cot, and shelves filled with his work. I was too naïve to understand the depth and range of what I was seeing. What I could recognize was his incredible technique. He could do feats of magic with clay. A women's skirt floating in the wind. A woman in high heels leaning against a wall. Three women in a market with baskets of fruit. He said his work was that of an artisan; it was anything but.

I brought him pictures of my work. Told him I would sweep his floors just for the chance to study him as he worked. Why he agreed, I can't imagine, but he did. Every Saturday morning I went to his studio, took in every flick of his fingers as if by watching I could replicate his technique. Of course, it wasn't possible—he was a master; I was not. Bruno evaluated artists on a scale of one to ten based on their fist, i.e., technique, intellect and soul. He believed I had a high rating where the soul and intellect were concerned, but needed a helluva lot of work on the fist.

I managed to get a show at a Madison Avenue gallery probably because the owners believed, what with my advertising connections, my work would sell. Mom told me about someone I grew up with who was somehow involved in the art world and suggested I invite her to see my work before the opening. I reconnected and she was all too happy to come by. Said she'd bring her mother who was the real art maven. I went on a high of anticipation. Within five minutes of their arrival they proceeded to shatter any illusions I had as to my abilities. In what can only be described as a battle to see who could render the most damage, they lashed out at me and my work for well over two hours. I was so stunned I didn't have the strength to ask them to leave. They finally departed but only when they were good and ready, their passions spent. When I finally got the strength to dial a phone, I called Dr. B. We spent the next weeks putting shattered me back together again. She attempted to convince me the decimation had nothing to do with my work and all to do with their relationship. I wanted to believe her, but the two women had spread glue onto my doubts, making them adhere to my gut. I didn't tell Mom of the visit, fearful she'd lose whatever faith in me she had.

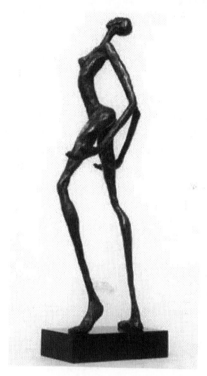

A Piece from Madison Ave. Show

On the night before the opening my Uncle Abe's wife called hysterically demanding to know what hospital my father had been taken to. I didn't know what she was talking about. "How could you not know?" she demanded. "What kind of mother do you have that she didn't call to tell you?"

I called every hospital in the city until I found he'd been admitted to Doctor's, but they wouldn't give me any information. I called my aunt back who then called my cousin who lived in my folks' building and learned of Dad's being taken out in an ambulance by the doorman. I grabbed a cab. My cousins drove over in their car. We arrived at the same time, our cars almost colliding. Mom exited the building and seeing all of us assumed something terrible had happened to my brother—who else was left? We managed to catch her before she fell to the ground in a faint. They kept Dad overnight even though it appeared to be a case of indigestion. Still, the scare was enough for my parents not to attend the opening and to cancel the planned after-party at their home. I had spent every night and weekend preparing for the show yet all I really remember is Dad sitting in the living room holding court for the few friends who came back with me to see how he was doing.

My Longest Affair

"You let him kill the kittens, Mom. Why the hell did you do that?"

"For heaven's sake, no one killed any kittens. It was our neighbor's cat. We were taking care of it while they were away. God, did you hold that against me all these years?"

"Of course not," I lie.

I have no idea if the kitten I believed to have been drowned by our neighbor's chauffer in Ossining—he told me that's what he had done—started my love affair with cats, but in 1968 I once again decided to adopt. Enter Socrates—a beautiful, blond tabby I'd rescued from the pound.

Soc and Me

Bored with his life in my studio apartment, or suffering from a vitamin deficiency, Socrates ate clothes—mine and anyone else's who stayed over. All too often I'd find the hem of my slacks with large sections missing, a sweater left on a chair chewed, socks and stockings torn apart. Still I was hooked. Watching a cat move, seeing him leap gracefully from one chair to the top of a shelf, or run under legs at a table with incredible fluidity, never ceased to amaze me. The vet suggested I get a second kitten to keep him busy, but it was a disaster. I came home to find the kitten cowering in a corner with Soc clearly ready for the kill. I returned the kitten and Soc continued his eating rampage.

On the anniversary of my sister's death, laid out with the flu, clothes off as the fever raged, I watched Socrates climb the curtains across from my bed and to my horror jump out the window which, according to cat safety rules, I'd only opened slightly from the top. He went straight down on to the concrete below. Throwing a coat over my naked body, my long hair looking like a crow's nest, I raced to the lobby, screaming for the doorman to help. I was convinced Soc had run away. (Amazing what denial will do to the brain.) The only way to reach him was through a first floor apartment window that opened onto the courtyard and occupied by two women who thankfully were at home. I climbed out their window still convinced he'd fled only to find him on the ground, alive, with blood spouting from his mouth. The women told me to go put on some clothes while they made a box for him. By the time I got back they had him and a cab waiting. I arrived at the Animal Hospital looking like a mad woman. My hair still not combed, my nose red from blowing, and blood on my hands and coat. As I raced up the ramp, coming towards me was one of my mother's friends. She was totally decked out, well groomed, with her poodle prancing beside her. Lord knows what she thought. Thankfully, Soc lived. The blood was from biting down on his tongue as he landed. His front leg was broken and set in a cast.

As if on cue "L" appeared in town that night. (No Black Orchid, but right on time. He would do the same the following year when I had to go to the Emergency Room with pleurisy—each rescue lengthening my attachment.) The vet advised Soc be kept in a cage when I was at the office so he wouldn't do more damage to himself. The thought of him locked up throughout the day too painful to imagine, I decided he'd come with me everywhere. We took the bus together in the morning, his front plastered paw resting on my shoulder as he nibbled away at my hair. At work, he managed to discover my boss's carpeted office which he preferred to the cold floors of mine. The tapping of his cast leg on the linoleum in the halls set off the rumors that my boss and I were back together. Nothing could have been further from the truth. Any involvement had ended the night he phoned at four in the morning rousing me from a deep sleep which stripped me of all guile.

"I'm in Hawaii. Definitely going to leave Emily. I'm coming home to marry you."

I let out one long, loud, visceral, "No!" and hung up. Then I sat upright in bed. My first proposal of marriage and I had not only refused, but was enormously relieved I had rejected him. One down, only "L" to go and the married man syndrome would be over. Ta Da!

Soc also accompanied me to the various recording studios that, thankful for my business, supplied us with kitty litter and water. On the day his cast came off I had a recording session with David Wayne (a wonderful actor, long passed, who played the original leprechaun in Finian's Rainbow on Broadway.) I took Soc with me one last time. By now David and Soc were pals, Soc playing around his feet. Suddenly David called out to us from the studio that Soc had disappeared. Everything stopped. I panicked and everyone began crawling around the studio searching for a sighting. Then, the engineer heard a sound coming from inside the console. He lifted the top and there, calmly wending his way around the intricate wires, was Soc! Too frightened to reach in, lest he get electrocuted, we held our breath until he finally walked out of an opening on the side. I snatched him up into my arms the way a mother grabs a child who makes it across a road filled with traffic. I wanted to kill him as did the head of the studio—Soc could have destroyed his sole means of support. Not to mention what it would have cost me in paying the damages. But at least he was alive.

Here I Go Again

Starting in the fall of 1968 a number of the top creative teams decided to go off on their own; some to form their own agencies; others to start production companies. There was even talk the agency was leaving its dingy digs at 42nd Street for Madison

Avenue. Then my boss, who somehow I still believed to be my protector, was let go. That he couldn't protect himself did not change how insecure I felt without him wandering the halls. No matter we'd hardly talked since my four in the morning scream. Or that he'd taken up with the receptionist, flaunting her by my office. I still believed him to be my mantle of protection. As for my own career, I knew I'd gone as far as I could go; from there on in it would be unending sameness. Besides, my identity was changing: from a radio producer who sculpted, to a sculptor who produced commercials to pay the rent. Unwittingly Dr. B had propelled me into my next career even though she desperately tried to talk me out of leaving the agency. We compromised. I would take a leave of absence, follow Bruno to Pietrasanta for the summer and when I returned, make up my mind.

There was a foundry in the town where Bruno went. I could cast my pieces there as well as have access to a studio. Luckily, my neighbor's daughter and husband had been looking for an apartment in the city, I offered up mine with the proviso they take care of Soc. They were more than willing especially as I would continue to pay the rent. I spent a few weeks trying to learn Italian; then broke the news to my parents. My father was furious.

"You're leaving a respectable job? For what?"

"I don't know if I'm leaving. I'm just taking a leave of absence."

"They'll fire you."

"No they won't."

"Now you think you're an artist? You'll be nothing."

Once again, Mother was torn and worried for me. But she attempted to placate Dad with, "It's only for two months, dear."

Seven days before I was to leave my brother-in-law married Marcia, a woman who would become the lynch pin of our family, and with whom I would spend my 50th birthday. The wedding was on the lawn of her home. No amount of good weather could lighten the spirits of many of the attendees. Three of Marcia's four children were miserable as she'd chosen to remarry only a few years after their father's death; my father looked as if he was being asked to bury his daughter again, Mother tried to make the best of it, happy for my brother-in-law, while acquiescing to my father's demand she not enjoy the day. My niece had hopes of gaining a mother; my nephew was thrilled he would have a brother and someone to call Mom, and I saw it as a new beginning. I was able to talk one of Marcia's daughters into leaving her room and joining the party. I spoke with Marcia's parents who were delighted their daughter would have a husband. I kibitzed with Chuck who was more than happy for our brother-in-law. And it was clear that Marcia accepted me as I was. For a brief moment I had a sense of self.

On the day I was to leave for Italy, Dorothy and my parents came to my apartment to see me off. Dad sulked, Dorothy tried to make conversation, Mom kept her visage neutral—once again in the middle. Whatever nerves I had about going were overridden by my desire to get the hell out of there. I hopped a cab and left them all in the street, Dorothy holding the sweater I had planned to wear on the plane.

Campo Italia

I spent the summer drawing from casts at the foundry, working on a new piece in a studio next to Jacques Lipshitz's, and waiting for a sign from the heavens—one that would tell me whether I should stay in Italy, return to the agency, or go home and sculpt full time. On an evening in a car with Gonzalo Fonseca—another well-known artist who was working there—lightning flashed on the mountain just as I told him about wanting a "sign." He said "There!" pointing at the lightning—leaving me to puzzle out what it meant. I knew I didn't possess the guts to stay and make my way alone in Italy, nor could I figure out the finances to do so, but I continued to play with the idea as if it were a real possibility.

One day towards the end of July, I received a letter from my tenants' parents. Soc had eaten their kids' clothes and they wanted out of our deal. Did I want to come home or should they drop him off at the ASCPA? I was not prepared to return, but if I didn't I'd be killing a perfectly healthy animal. Guilty as hell over my selfishness I wrote a tear streaked letter asking my neighbor to find a home for Soc and prayed it wouldn't be the ASPCA. Then, almost on cue, at the end of August, I packed up and returned home. (Incredibly, my neighbor took Soc to his factory where Soc turned into the perfect mouser. Eventually he was sent upstate to live out his life on a farm.)

For Better or for Worse

There was no turning back. I was on to career number three. Dr. B did not hide her dismay. My mind made up, I gave notice. Mac Dane (the Dane of Doyle Dane Bernbach) took pity and fired me so I could collect unemployment; Bernbach told me to come by for bagels and cream cheese whenever I was hungry which he clearly expected I would be; and my father once again refused to talk with me, furious I could actually leave a job where I was respected. More to the point, leave a job about which he could boast.

Unlike my transition from acting to radio producer which evolved over time, I hurtled towards my next career without a thought as to how I'd support myself. Clearly whatever savings I had would not last long—DDB had not paid well. So Dr. B was out—therapy was for a working stiff, not a starving artist. Besides, the fear that curing my neurosis would destroy whatever talent I had, had never left even though it was therapy and Dr. B that led me to study. Someone suggested I reach out to the Creatives who formed their own production companies in the hopes they'd hire me to work as an extra in their commercials. I was, after all, still a member of SAG and AFTRA, never having resigned from either union. The first person I called told me to use his name and speak to his casting director. I hung up the phone, dialed, and before she had the chance to say more than hello, I blabbered how I was a sculptor and while I didn't want to steal work from real actors, I had studied acting, worked as an actor, was union and knew how to behave on a set.

Her answer, "I know you can act, Margo, saw every show you were in at BU."

Incredibly we'd been classmates, I just didn't know her by her married name. From then on I had a source of income, although not steady, but enough to extend my unemployment insurance and provide me with health insurance (to this day.) There is nothing more boring than sitting on a set for hours waiting for the few seconds when you're needed to fill in the background of a shot. But over time, those of us who were hired became like family and days passed quickly enough. However, when I got work with other companies, life wasn't as pleasant. Were there moments when the acting bug reemerged and I sat on a set hoping to be "discovered" or at least upgraded to a principal? Absolutely! More than one. But I had a new goal and I neither was, nor am, capable of striving for more than one goal at a time.

I signed up for drawing classes at the Art Students League. The Peace and Civil Rights Movements were in full force, and convinced artists would be the first ones out in front, I attempted to round up students to join the various marches. I hung posters on all the bulletin boards and was surprised as well as dismayed at the lack of interest. "We're artists. No time for politics," I would be told as I tried to enlist classmates to the cause. And here I'd assumed artists were of a higher moral character than those of us in advertising. Granted there we'd protested from the safety of a recording studio, but at least we protested. Then came the day I was called into the head of the school's office.

"You have to stop your activities or leave the school."

I couldn't believe what was occurring. Marching for peace was radical? A few days later I was contacted by the SDS to join them. I decided art willed out and while I marched in both New York and D.C., I remained at the league for one more semester where I became friends with Lynne Mayo—another sculptor. Over time I poured out my insecurities as to my abilities and she suggested I study under her former teacher up at Columbia. I enrolled there, but not before I adopted Pablo—a beautiful tabby named for Casals not Picasso—the emptiness of the apartment without another living creature too much to bear.

One Foot In; One Foot Out

I found an apartment relatively near the campus—well, in reality, about thirty blocks away—a two bedroom on a low floor in the back of a doorman building on 77th Street just off Riverside Drive. I had forgotten how cold and windy Riverside Drive could be with its proximity to the Hudson River. I shouldn't have. Years before I'd been blown ten blocks down the drive, my feet literally off the ground until I could grab on to a lamppost- my school books and shoes flying off into the wind. Thankfully a truck driver saw me, pulled over, tied a rope around his waist, attached the other end of the rope to his truck, then braved the storm to get to me and pull me to safety.

Because my apartment faced a courtyard, the rent was relatively cheap. I could never tell if it was morning or night, warm or cold. Many a day I ran downstairs only to find it had snowed and I was dressed for spring. It's incredible I was not kicked out of the building. This was a relatively upscale building into which I hauled huge bags of plaster, bins of clay and large pieces of stone. I put my bed in the rear room, a butcher block table in the middle one for chipping away at alabaster, and the two *Naugahyde* love seats my mom helped me purchase in the living room. Eventually these were shoved aside to make room for an enormous sculpture. It survived only to be photographed; then it was destroyed. Like a cat who wanted to be on both sides of a door at the same time, I was not ready to place both my feet in the art world and find a real studio in a loft building.

Vera's Kids on Riverside Drive Sculpture

I made three enduring friendships that year: the first, a stay-at-home mom who took pity on her single neighbor downstairs and often brought dinner to my door. Vera was also an admirer of anyone who had a creative bone in her body, swearing she didn't possess one. I knew she was born in Czechoslovakia, but never questioned her about her early years until one evening, after returning my dinner plate, I watched her scrub the dining room floor on her hands and knees for the second time in two days. I made some off-hand remark to her husband about overdoing cleanliness. "I thought you knew," he said and went on to explain that she, her mother and older sister were imprisoned in Theresienstadt, the Nazi concentration camp that masqueraded to the world as a place where music was played and children drew. Her job there: to scrub floors. One would think it would be the last thing she would do, and yet there she was, still on her hands and knees every night after dinner. I never could discern whether it was a habit instilled in childhood, or she believed her survival still depended on a clean floor.

Many years later, I visited Vera and her husband in Washington, DC to find much of my work occupying their walls and mantle. I knew they had bought pieces from me over the years, but their apartment felt like the Krasne museum. On the same visit, Vera took me to the Holocaust museum. I already knew she never spoke with her mother and sister of what went on in the camp, so I didn't feel I could pry. Vera's manner of speech could be abrupt, verging on the dismissive, and I allowed her to take the lead of what we could or could not comment on. When we reached the box car, a replica of the transport in which Jews were herded to the camps, she said as blithely as if she were pointing to a corner table at a restaurant, "That's where my mother, sister and I sat." I wanted to ask her what else she remembered, but remained mute. She had been, after all, only six. Besides, what was there to ask? I'd read enough books on the holocaust. I kept my top teeth pressed into my lower lip. When we arrived at the exhibit of Theresienstadt children's drawings, I mimicked her off-hand manner.

"So where's yours?" I asked.

"I told you I wasn't creative!" her reply. I can't imagine what anyone who heard us must have thought.

We were now at a wall with the names of the cities and their populations of those rounded up. She searched for hers and I wondered why she hadn't found it before. Then she sent me to watch alone the film of the survivors. I finally had the privacy to weep. After years of being in a family where anything German was verboten, Vera was the first Jew I'd met who drove a VW and told me to buy German goods. "Listen! The better they do, the more money we get. So, go! Buy!" Her attitude towards all things German would come in handy later in more ways than one.

The second friendship was with Margaret Worth, a painter from Australia. She was going for her Masters in Art and dating our instructor—the teacher Lynne had recommended. Friends warned Margaret he would make a lousy husband, but she married him anyway. She would become my emotional support; I her rescuer and her daughter's Godmother.

And the third friendship: the Dishys. A couple, who, with their two children, became like family in years when I desperately needed one. It would be Bernard Dishy who threatened to murder Uncle Murray if he'd been alive. Both Linda and Bernie took an interest in my work, becoming much valued and needed patrons as well as friends.

All In

When classes ended, it became clear I needed a space more suited to my work. Once again Lynne Mayo stepped in with a lead to a loft on Bond Street. While the owners would supply the materials, if I wished to rent a floor, I'd have to make it livable. This meant plastering the 11 ft. ceiling (all 2000 sq. ft. of it,) painting the entire loft, installing the wiring, plumbing, etc. With the rent at $300 a month not due until the plumbing was installed—I jumped at the chance. Little did I know what the renovations would entail.

Bond Street runs all of two blocks—from Broadway to the Bowery two blocks north of Houston. Today it is two of the "hot" blocks in the city. In the early 1970's it was bereft of any amenities, having gone through the typical New York City cycle: first, the affluent lay claim, then leave for greener pastures, after which the wannabes move in and out as they doggedly follow the climbers, light industry inhabits the empty spaces, the neighborhood disintegrates affording cheap spaces for artists who move in, invite the wealthy over as potential patrons, the wealthy find the artists' spaces alluring, move in, remodel and destroy the very atmosphere which had attracted them in the first place.

24 Bond was bought as an income producing venture by three artists. Joseph Kosuth—at the time Leo Castelli's "it" minimalist who laid claim to the third floor. Alex Hay—another minimalist who had worked with, and for, Merce Cunningham—and who supposedly Kosuth had staked to the second floor with the proviso Alex would oversee the building's renovation. And last, Virginia Admiral, who owned the sixth. All but Alex planned to rent out their spaces. (Rumor had it Virginia slept in a bathtub in her office blocks away. Whether or not this was true, I have no idea. What I now know was she was an artist in her own right and mother of the actor Robert deNiro.) Eventually Robert Mapplethorpe bought, lived and worked on the 5th floor. He was one of the gentlest men I have ever met—in sharp contrast to his implicit sexual photographs which were designed to shock all sensibilities, and certainly did mine, as did the large gold leafed swastika he hung right across from the elevator. His was a transom I could not cross. They all owned a share of my floor as well as the ground floor store and

basement rented out to Sam Rivers, an avant-garde jazz musician, his wife Bea, their children, grandchildren and three large German Shepherds. Studio Rivbea, as it was known, became the gathering place for musicians. For the rest of us, the sounds that emanated well into the early morning hours on Saturday nights and during the two weeks of the Newport Jazz Festival made our lives hell. Bea worked at AT&T to support the clan and couldn't get through a sentence without the "F" word taking the place of adverbs, adjectives and conjunctions as well as periods and commas. I constantly wondered what it was like for her at the office.

My loft was approximately 100' long and 20' wide with windows and fire escapes in front and back. I put bars on the rear ones, assuming the front would be safe as it faced the street. For months my only source of electricity was supplied by a photographer in the next building who ran a cable from his loft through my side window and loaned me one of his huge studio lamps until another artist, who made his living as an electrician—also a Lynne contact—donated his time and laid the wiring in spite of one limp arm the result of his having been electrified on a job. Alex, true to his word if not our time-frame, installed the plumbing. Luckily my lease was not up at 77th Street for a few weeks so I had a place to retreat to; the trio up on the sixth floor was not as lucky. They had to camp out.

Working on a ceiling is hard enough for a well-built man, but almost impossible for a woman with little upper body strength and I had (have) little or none. But priding myself on having mastered the art of mixing plaster, I did not realize I could use a retardant to slow the process thus enabling larger amounts to be mixed at a time. (If ready mixed plaster was available at the time, no one mentioned it to me.) So, every day I climbed my newly purchased 10' ladder, scraped a section, climbed down, mixed, climbed up and applied. Most evenings I'd collapse without food unless Vera appeared with a tray. One night, for the first and only time since

I was seven, exhausted beyond anything I'd known, I wet my bed. Even though I woke up before permanently damaging the mattress, the shame was overwhelming. Now, I have always dealt with angst by blabbing to anyone who will listen until, like rain, my anxiety begins to evaporate as it lands on another's shoulders. This time I chose the safest ones: Dorothy's. She told her husband, an ex-marine, and he absolved me. "Grown men wet their beds in basic training—nothing to be ashamed of."

Clearly I couldn't do this alone. Trouble was the pickings were limited as most people I knew had day jobs. Finally, I found a volunteer. A lovely man though physically lacking in construction skills. It took him three days to learn how to mix a decent bucket. Just as he handed it to me, with a look of trepidation and pride, there were screams outside my stairwell door pleading for help. I considered pretending I wasn't home, but the voice—only partially recognizable as Jim's, one of my six floor neighbors—was in such distress, I had no choice but to relinquish the bucket, climb down and go to the door. It was Jim, ashen beyond pale, holding up a young man covered in blood, his arm partially severed. Through their sobs I learned they'd been dismantling their metal ceiling, a section had fallen off and sheared the young man's arm through to the bone. Without a phone—no lines yet installed and obviously no cell phones—the only way to get help was to make their way down the stairs to my floor.

I learned something about myself that day: I am great in an emergency as long as, instinctively, I know there's no one around who's emotionally stronger. My friend, the mixer, had turned ghastly white and stood frozen with bucket in hand, and my upstairs neighbor was too far gone to think straight. I ordered him to run to a phone booth three blocks away, used the scarf I'd wrapped around my head as a tourniquet and held the young man and his arm together—as well as myself—until help arrived. Amazingly he survived, arm attached.

With all the sex I indulged in, I was still bloody naïve. I knew Jim was gay, and automatically assumed the couple he'd moved in with were straight. Feeling guilty that I still had an apartment with heat and electricity, I invited them to stay with me at night on Riverside Drive. The noises emanating from the room next to mine dispelled all assumptions. It was a true ménage-a-trois. I was incensed at their not maintaining some sort of decorum as guests in my home, and told them to cool it or find another place to stay. They chose not to return. (In retrospect, it's incredible how prudish and judgmental I was about others' behavior and yet managed totally to rationalize my own. I can only explain it, if it needs explaining, that one part of my brain had adopted my parents mores while the other part allowed me to be very much a part of the newly sexually liberated world of the late sixties and early seventies.)

Kosuth had rented his floor to a sexually provocative, attractive photographer and his wife. With a head start, they'd managed to install a shower, kitchen and darkroom while I was still plastering the ceiling. They also had live-in help—a young man with whom they exchanged room and board for work even though he was usually stoned. When finally my lease at Riverside Drive was up, I had no choice but to move into the loft, and like the sixth floor trio began scrounging for showers. (I stayed away from my folks' place having no desire to fuel my father's wrath as to just how far I'd fallen.) The photographer's wife had a job and therefore not home during the day. I visited some evenings as she sat in a rocking chair knitting in a long denim skirt, her hair straight down her back as if Haight-Ashbury had moved east. They offered me use of their shower, and not wanting to take advantage I tried to keep my visits to a minimum, wrapping myself in a large towel, running downstairs to lather up, wash off and head back to my floor. One time I exited the shower stall to find the photographer waiting half-naked outside. As I said he was extremely attractive and

I succumbed all too readily. Thankfully it was lousy sex—there's rough and then there's really rough—during which he informed me he was also screwing the guy staying with them as part of the deal. Somehow knowing that eradicated any guilt I felt at betraying his wife's kindness. I found other places to shower only dropping by every so often for a cup of tea in the evening so she wouldn't take my sudden disappearance as reason to suspect what had occurred. As I said, it was the Seventies.

Mom informed me that Dad had made my brother drive him to see where I was living. "He was very upset, dear. You know, it looks just like the tenements he spent years escaping." And it did look like a tenement. As for the neighborhood, it was loaded with bums' bodies—ones we had to climb over in order to make our way to LaGuardia Place where we could get groceries and do laundry. I had heard stories of people dropping baskets on long ropes out of windows so Dad and his brothers could deliver their wares when they arrived in New York, but at Bond Street there was no such thing as deliveries. And our freight elevator was both a Godsend and nuisance for those of us on the upper floors. When we needed to leave the building, we had to find someone willing to take it. If there were no takers, we had to lock it up on our own floor, and upon our return climb the stairs to retrieve it so we could ride it down to pick up whatever supplies we were bringing in.

I had begged Alex to install a shower rather than a tub—the specter of Dad standing outside the bathroom door having left me loathe to soaking. But Alex had refused. Still, when I could finally bathe in my own place, I immersed myself into the water as if at a luxurious spa. It didn't last long. The bathroom had a window. And there, waving, grinning, making lewd gestures stood a group of workmen on an adjoining fire escape. I decided to hell with it and sunk deeper into the water. I put sheets up over the window the next day, but the bathtub became a place to wash up, not relax in.

Bond Street was now my symbolic commitment to diving headlong into the art world even though I was plagued with doubts as to my actual talent. I had no problem calling myself a sculptor. It's what I did. But "Artist?" Artists were society's outliers, whereas I knew which side of the plate the fish fork went and still served friends off Wedgwood dishes I'd bought in London. And although I dressed in the hippie style of the day, I did it with a self-conscious awareness that it wouldn't fly in my parents' world. In my desperation for reassurance I drove friends crazy besieging them to look at my work, the same way I'd begged my High School sculpting teacher, Peter Haywood. "Is it good? Am I?"

By now I did have a better grasp of drawing, though it would be a long time before I found my way onto the paper with abandoned control. It would take trying my hand at lithographs for it all to coalesce. Something about putting my crayon onto the stone allowed me to feel the depth of the paper. For the first time, drawing made sense. Still I realized I needed to study anatomy. So, in typical fashion, rather than take a course, I decided to teach it. I called a few friends; asked if they, or someone they knew, would like to sign up for a drawing class and, amazingly, got a number of takers. With Bridgeman's Drawing from Life, Grey's Anatomy, and another book on artist's anatomy, I managed to stay one step ahead of my so-called students. A few years later, I would produce a piece so anatomically correct, yet in a position physically impossible for the human body to achieve, that even Bruno Lucchesi questioned me as to whether I had cast off a body or used a model. My "fist" went way up in his estimation.

Lucchesi's Surprise

On the other hand the flat canvas remained elusive. Large
spaces required large pieces and I bought paint, yards of canvas
that I stretched over 4' x 8' two-by-fours hammered together, and

started in. I am anything but a colorist and in retrospect could have saved time, energy and funds by simply staying with black, white and grey. Of course, once again, I chose as my subject a large woman. That she filled the canvas in the most grotesque manner, a flying buttress coming at the viewer, concerned me, but my mind wasn't on her as much as the paint. I couldn't make it work no matter how I struggled. Change a color here, and the rest of the canvas went into turmoil. Still, I refused to give up. As my gargoyle didn't work on the canvas itself, I decided she had to leave it. I kept seeing a hand and foot emerging into three dimensional space. Anyone in their right mind would have simply returned to sculpting, but no, I now had something to prove. I was going to combine the two mediums not in a bas relief, but with canvas, paint and what? Plaster? Too heavy.

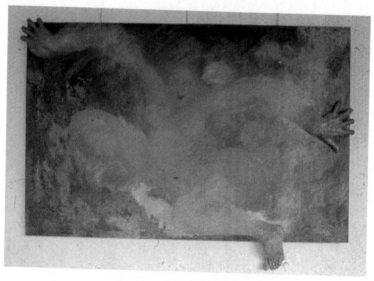

First Woman Emerging

Lynne suggested acrylic and fiber glass. And so it started. Figures emerging from canvases. The first few ghastly; the next – when I stopped worrying about color and focused on the drawing—better; until they were each unique. I even began to create three dimensional drawings of the figure. Always women trying to break free. Read what you wish into my choices. I didn't see them as being replicas of myself, certainly not my exterior. But interior? Definitely. I had internalized Graham's movements. Whatever I had experienced in Martha's classes by attempting to master her deep contractions and expansive releases were now internalized to such an extent that they made their way into the work itself.

Fourth Emerging Woman

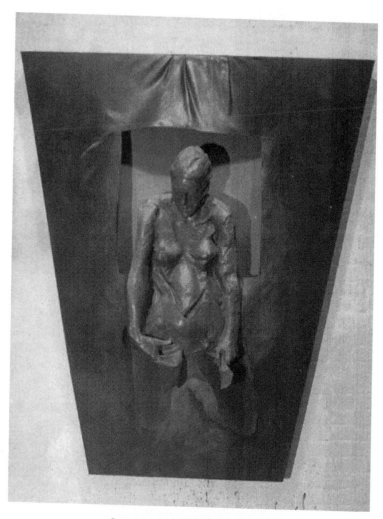

Seventh Woman Emerging

Always on the lookout for someone who could help me, Mom told me of another woman from 275 CPW—this one a contemporary of my siblings—who was now an art dealer buying and selling corporate art. I never told Mom about the mother/daughter team who had all but eviscerated me and I was leery of trying again. Eventually though my need to get a dealer outweighed any anxieties and I invited her down. The first meeting could only be described of one of intense relief on both our parts: hers from seeing the work was of a high caliber; mine that history didn't repeat itself. My work being anything but what corporations wanted for their walls, she couldn't place it, but she did become an emotional support, often took me to dinner—even going so far as to buying one of my paper montages which she hung over her bed. Still, I could never quell my yearning for her to do more.

For reasons no longer remembered, I left the human figure and turned to the horse. It was not that I rode, or was ever a rider. My equestrian abilities sorely lacking—sore being more than the appropriate word. My year of the horse coincided with the year the First Women's Bank was to open on 57th Street off Park Avenue. It actually was a first: women in charge of their and other people's money. Someone suggested I contact them. Desperate for the work to be seen, I offered the managers the chance to borrow any piece they'd like for as long as they'd like. They were more than amenable and chose for their main room Horses Rearing. It was a painted work 8' high x 4' wide x 2' deep of two horses emerging from the canvas as they reared up towards each other. I was ecstatic. Finally, the world would see my work. I called everyone. But once again, disappointment waited. The piece hung at the bank for all of two weeks until Molly Parnas, a member of their Board, obviously unaware of how horses procreate, assumed they were copulating and ordered them removed. (And this after all her dresses my mom and sister had bought!) As I plunged into another funk, friends assured me I'd get a second chance somewhere else. I had no reason to believe them.

HORSES REARING—not copulating

There came a day when I had to pick Mom up at the hospital after undergoing surgery-for what I don't remember—and take Dad in for testing. In between the three of us had lunch at their apartment. Dad was already upset with me as he had wanted me to live with him during Mother's hospital stay. He had called at all hours of the day and night, pleading with me to move in with him. This in spite of the fact he liked the young woman my brother had found to stay with him. Over lunch I mentioned a friend had taken up numerology and that she'd sworn my luck would change if I replaced my middle initial "J" with a "T." Mom and I could see his fury start. "Give up my name?" he cried. Mom, who could enjoy a bit of magical thinking, tried to calm him down by explaining the "J" was for her mother Jennie, not for him, and if she didn't care, neither should he. He got so upset we were afraid he'd have a heart attack right then and there. I told him to forget it—the "J" would stand.

The next few weeks were harrowing. A transformer in an AT&T station had blown and none of us had working phones. AT&T set up a bank of telephone booths a few blocks away and I would race to call home to see how Dad was doing. If Mother needed to reach me, she would call a friend whose phone was working and someone would find a way to either come down to give the message, sometimes by calling the hardware store. By now, Dad was now somewhere between eighty-eight and ninety—his birth date never recorded. He was in the last stages of his illness. We had thought it was his heart, but turned out he'd had a malignant tumor behind his esophagus which his doctor had decided years earlier not to treat. One afternoon, Mom and I arrived at his hospital bed to find him weak, desperate, furious. An intern had disobeyed orders and forced a blood transfusion on him in the middle of the night. Mom went to his bedside. I stood near the door, still persona non grata—this time for not moving in with Mom while he was hospitalized.

"Look! Look what they've done to me. Get me out of here!" he cried. He was emaciated, his arms black and blue, veins popping out yet collapsed. We ordered a hospital bed for the house, nurses around the clock, an ambulance, and home he came. Persona non grata or not—I was there daily. A few days later when my brother, brother-in-law and his wife were to visit, Dad indicated he was too tired.

"I'll call and tell them not to come," I said.

His eyes raged fury. "Did I tell you to?"

"I just thought ..."

Mom and I waited for what would come next. He surprised us both. Quietly, as if all anger had suddenly been drained from him, he told me to, "Go! Tell them tomorrow."

Days later, with the whole family present, Dad went into a weird euphoria. He danced around the room in his bathrobe and slippers—the navy blue Sulka robe—handing each of us a rose from a vase someone had sent—and demanded kisses. Then he took to his bed.

In the months leading up to Dad's death, I had begun to let Mom into my life. No big flinging open of what it was like to be me. No conscious divulgences, but I would tell her about an argument I'd had with a friend, then wait to see whose side she would take. When it was mine, I felt safe enough to test again. Not immediately—perhaps a few weeks later. I'd talk about a gallery rejection or a buyer who hadn't shown. Each time I expected her disapproval or disappointment. It never came.

We were now waiting for Dad to die. Mom spent most of the time prone on the pull out sofa in the den; Dad ensconced in their room with nurses around the clock. I went back and forth between them. Now, this may seem strange, but neither Mom nor I owned a black dress—standard garb for New York City women. I still dressed as a hippie—sandals and to-the-floor paisley skirts; and

Mom had stopped wearing black when my sister had ordered us not to in the months before she died—going so far as to make Mom get rid of those she owned. (Two days before my sister's funeral, my Aunt Mary had bought each of us one. We lived in them for days, then cut them up, and threw them away.) This time we were going to be a bit more prepared—though not by much. I was getting ready to leave to go black dress shopping when the phone rang. It was Dorothy.

"'L's' in town looking for you."

Mom knew of "L" as Dorothy's old friend and someone I sometimes hung out with. But true to form, I had never let her in on the real relationship.

"Tell "L" I'll be home later this evening. He can call me then," I told Dorothy.

"He can call you here," Mom said. "It's not a problem."

I said good-bye to Dorothy, turned to Mom and with no filter on my thoughts, let out the truth. "There's no way I'm going to have an old lover call here when we haven't spoken in ages."

And how did Mom respond? Well, it was a good thing she was lying down or she would have passed out on the floor "But I always told your father you were a good girl," she gasped.

I let out a loud guffaw. "I am a good girl. If I were still a virgin at 37 then you'd really have something to worry about." I stood up to get my coat.

She stopped me with, "If he were single, would you have married him?" That was my Mom. When there was no need of pretense, she took life as it came.

Without any apologies, I answered, "No way. I prefer to be the one cheating, not the one cheated upon."

I got to the front door as my brother arrived. I couldn't stop giggling. Thirty seven years and we finally had a conversation about sex. Not the act itself, but a part of my life never even touched upon before in conversation. "Good luck." I told him. "She just found out I'm not a virgin." Then I grabbed my coat and was out of there. I couldn't wipe the grin off my face for hours after. The cat was out of the bag and I was finally free to be me.

Dad's final hours were a battle with the Gods. I was at his bedside as the death rattle filled the room. Then just at the moment I turned away, he was gone. I went into Mom. She was strangely calm. Then I called the doctor who arrived to pronounce him dead. Death certificate signed, two men in black suits came to wheel the body away, black bag and all. They looked like Mutt and Jeff as drawn by Charles "Chas" Adams. I almost burst out laughing. At three in the morning I returned home at the same time my neighbor, Helen, who lived in the building next door, was coming back from a night out.

"My Dad just died and I'm going to break open a bottle of scotch. Want to join?"

Turned out her dad had died the year before and, to top it off, she and her husband had separated.

"I have one piece of advice for you," she said as we knocked off the third refill.

"I'll take whatever you have to give."

"You are going to have one helluva year. There will be times you will do something that convinces you you've gone mad. You haven't. It's par for the course. Just go with it. It's okay."

I had no idea what she was talking about. Dad was finally gone. No more wars. No more confrontations. I couldn't imagine what could be crazier than what I had already been through.

"And one more thing. You'll be going along and everything will seem great and suddenly it will hit you like a wave. And there you'll be—maybe in the middle of a street—sobbing."

She was right on all counts.

As I said, Mom and I could pick up a conversation laid down days, months, even years earlier. This one occurred three days after Dorothy's phone call. In between Dad had died, we'd held his funeral and sat Shiva. I arrived at Mom's apartment and found her standing on her little terrace. I could never go out on it with her. The height scared me, but Mom loved it. She came back into the room saying it would be perfect if she could have grass on the tiny terrace's floor. I knew she meant Astro-turf and thought I could find her a piece. I'd maintained a friendship of sorts with my ex-boss from the ad agency. He and the woman he'd been seeing had mentioned they'd used Astro-turf in their country home. I called hoping they had some left over. They didn't. When I hung up, Mom, as if not a minute had passed from when she lay prone on the sofa bed days earlier, said, "And Don too?"

"I'm not answering that, Mom."

"I'm asking."

"And I'm not answering."

A moment or two passed. Then,

"What about Harvey B?"

I couldn't believe it. She went on to list every man I had ever mentioned even in passing. She pulled up names I had long forgotten—a question mark after each. I left the room on some excuse and the conversation was dropped. It amazed me how long she'd maintained a blind eye while seeing my life exactly as it was. Almost as an apology one day, in one of our many phone calls, she confessed, "You know, your father loved your sister more than anything or anyone—which is why I became her best friend." I stood transfixed staring at the receiver in my hand. Is that what had set off the entire family dynamic? My father's unabashed love of his first born? How sad for all concerned.

At some point the trio on the sixth floor broke up and moved out and a painter moved in. He had been reworking the same eight 10' by 4' woodcut panels for well over ten years and took the loft not to live in, but to finish them. I am not sure if he ever did. One afternoon, about three months after Dad died, I left my loft to shop and deposited the elevator with the "woodcutter" who promised to be around when I got back. Arms loaded with groceries, I rang for the elevator. Suddenly the Rivers' door opened and out leapt their three untrained, unchained German shepherds. They made their way straight for me. One put his teeth around my ankle, one on my wrist, and another stood on his back legs directly behind me, his front paws on my shoulders and panted into my ear. Any thoughts, once harbored, I could be another St. Francis of Assisi evaporated. I had no doubts that if I moved a muscle, I would be ripped to shreds. I heard the elevator descend, saw it come into view through the glass door and in the most controlled voice I could muster; I called out to the painter that the dogs were on me. The painter started making weird sounds and banging on the elevator door. It distracted them just long enough so he could simultaneously swing open the door and pull me to safety. I don't think I've ever been as grateful. That night a bum climbed through my front window—probably looking for a place to sleep. My screams chased him away.

That same week my brother's wife, who lived in an upscale home in Westchester, was awakened to find three strange men in her room. Alone in the house—my brother in Vegas gambling—she hollered bloody murder, pressed the panic button by her bed, and, incredibly, the men left without the piles of silver they'd accumulated downstairs. My brother-in-law drove over and stayed with her until my brother and the live-in couple who took care of the house returned. I am not saying what my sister-in-law endured wasn't scary as hell, but all I heard from my mother was, "Poor Mickey, what she's going through, poor Mickey, poor poor Mickey."

For the first and only time in my life, I exploded at Mom. "Enough with Mickey! She has help. She's fine. She's not alone. I was attacked by three dogs and a man climbed in here , I have no help, work like crazy for whatever money I have, so enough with poor Mickey!" Then, in a state of total shock at what I had just done, fully expecting all hell to break loose. I hung up and waited. When a few minutes later the phone rang, I could barely pick it up.

"I think from now on I should be open to hearing what's going on with you," she said. The old days definitely were over. We were moving on. Clearly we were both rewriting the rules.

———

If I wanted heat—which I did, my body temperature always being on the cold side—it was up to me to tend to the furnace. Not that the others in the building, including Alex and Robert, didn't enjoy their creature comforts, they just didn't want to wait for the repairman when the furnace glitched. (It was also possible they were too stoned to notice the cold.) Eventually my chores were shared by another photographer who took over the lease from the first. We became friends. Stan did not have a roving eye—he was involved with his work and committed to his wife. Besides, by the time they moved in, I had promised myself no more bedding anyone on home turf.

My cousin Estelle's daughter called asking if I knew of a darkroom she could use. We hadn't spoken in years as she had moved to Israel where she'd taken up photography. I put her in touch with

Stan. She came by for a sort of a belated condolence call. Naturally we talked about my Dad. She'd assumed he'd left me money. I explained there was nothing to leave. Whatever monies there were Mom needed to live on. Still Gail was incensed. I found the visit strange as well as confusing when she mentioned she was in town not only to visit her folks, but to make out a will. I couldn't understand why anyone our age, and obviously not successful, would need to do so. Besides, I told her, I had my inheritance, I'd given up smoking. It would be a few more years before I'd understand what different places we'd been coming from.

The materials I had chosen to create my three dimensional canvases turned out to be highly toxic. It wasn't until rumors started about Larry Rivers having a liver or kidney disease, did I consider changing mediums or, at the very least, donning protective gear. I bought goggles to keep the fiberglass out of my eyes. I tried a face mask but found it suffocating. As for ventilation, it was too cold to work with the windows open. The one material I did give up was asbestos which I'd been mixing into the resin to make it thicker— another Lynne Mayo tip—then grinding it down once it dried. Somehow Virginia Admiral (again, deNiro's mother and one of my landlords) got wind and called saying she'd throw me out if I didn't stop. Between the fumes and fiberglass—not to mention the cigarettes I'd inhaled over the years—I'd unwittingly laid the groundwork for the lousy lungs to come. Looking back, I wonder if the danger of it all was to prove to myself that maybe, just maybe, I was an artist willing to sacrifice my health for art.

The following winter proved to be the hardest yet. I got flu after flu, a case of the crabs—two weeks after a one-night stand had called to tell me I had given it to him—and my cousin Gail secured a one-woman show at the Jewish Museum. I was filled with resentment. How could she who had just taken up photography land a gallery whereas I'd been working at my art for years? Was this another cousin with all the luck? Of course, I had no choice but to show up. It would have been unseemly not to. But I did it with my anger visible. It was photography for Christ's sake! Not art! The gallery was crowded with friends and family. And there were huge prints on every wall. My anger not abated when friends reminded me that Van Gogh had never sold a painting. At least his brother took care of him, I'd counter, paid for him to continue; mine just thought I was a neurotic mess. Every slight, real or imagined, fueled my bitterness. I was now in a constant state of rage.

Kosuth sold his floor and Stan and his wife bought and moved to a loft a block away. The new owners convinced the other three to increase my rent to $400.00 with the proviso I also take care of the building. Their gluttony more than I could take, I decided not to renew my lease and began the search for a new home. This time Mom put me in touch with a son of a friend who headed a large real estate firm in the city and who found the loft on 20th Street. Every day I wheeled a shopping cart filled with miscellany from Bond Street up to 20th. When my Bond Street lease was up, it was time to move. Riding in the last of the three truckloads filled with my work and machinery, we turned the corner onto Third Avenue and I watched a man hang up a string of pennants announcing a grocery store opening. More years would pass for Bond Street to morph into what it is today, but those flags were the first sign of its renaissance.

A year later, at one in the morning, as I cleared dishes from a birthday party I'd thrown myself, the phone rang. It was Mapplethorpe. "Marg, I smell smoke," he said. "Do you?" Whether he was on drugs or suffering from AIDS from which he died, I'll never know. I told him, I'd moved out a year before and he apologized and hung up. My connection to Bond Street had officially ended.

The Beginning of This End

I had sworn off toxic materials and began working in wax. I found it too unstable and switched to terra cotta—all the while still trying to paint. I installed a kiln—cutting down on casting costs—and began firing my pieces having no idea of whether or not it could prove dangerous. My work now could be said to be more mature, still based on the figure, but far more abstract. Whatever money I earned—from the odd jobs such as painting someone's apartment, working as an extra in a commercial, maître d'ing at a friend's restaurant and sometimes selling a drawing or sculpture—went back mostly into materials, casting, and photographing the work. I lived frugally to the point of extreme cheapness.

As I said, my relationship with money had always been a bit skewed. I would walk miles to save ten cents per pound on a chicken while handing over hundreds to a foundry even without having a buyer for my work, or a gallery in which to show it. That said, I had a small stash that no one knew of—a pittance of a savings account I would add to no matter how dire things seemed. My brother did finally buy a piece and sometimes wrote a check for $200.00 for my birthday. That too got saved.

In the meantime, I schlepped slides of my work—all we had back then—to gallery after gallery. If I was with a male friend, the gallery owner looked at his work and ignored mine. Still, I kept at it putting on a front that all was right with my world. (Lynne Mayo once told me of a minimalist who described an artist as someone who opens his window, yells, "Fuck you!" then slams it shut, his whole body quaking. It was how I felt.) In many ways, I had traded aspects of the acting world I despised for those of the art world. In the first I silently screamed, "Look at me!" "Hire me!" "Recognize me!!!" at anyone with a connection to the theater. In this world it was, "Buy my work!" "Show my work" "Love my work." Whether "me" or "my" it was still: I! I! I!

When I'd been at the agency, I took vacations. If you didn't take the days, you lost them. Now, with limited funds, I rarely went away. Certainly not on any regular basis. But every few years, the sameness of my surroundings, of my life, would overwhelm and I'd leave town with very little planning. It was as if I were the steam from a kettle filled with boiling water, the bubbles propelling me out of town. I'd find a cheap hotel on one of the Islands—usually St. Thomas—dig into my savings, and escape. The first two days always were misery as I felt painfully alone, but eventually I'd find a couple who were willing to have me tag along and the week would actually be rejuvenating. On one of these vacations, I met a couple from Virginia. We stayed in touch and on March 11th, 1978 the wife came to New York to visit. I was in another one of my deep lows and as I remember the evening, she kindly listened to my depressive rant, and decided to buy a drawing. Feeling somewhat rejuvenated, I re-entered the loft a little before 11 PM, and resolved to get my act together. I picked up a paint brush—I was now playing with washed canvases—and automatically turned on the TV for background noise. As the sound came up I heard Walter Cronkite's voice announce, "The body found shot to death on the beach outside of Tel Aviv today before the bus hijacking is that of Gail Rubin from New York."

My cousin! The daughter who had lived one floor above me on Fifth Avenue, the ethereal blonde who had the show at the Jewish Museum, the child I had played with in the sand box—had been shot in the head by a dark haired Palestinian beauty of the same age. Stunned and furious, all at the same time, I called Mom demanding to know why I had to hear the news from a television set. In what can only be called Jewish comic relief she said she had not wanted to upset me, "I thought you should get a good night sleep before I told you."

Had Gail and I been close? No. But we had sewn a new relationship when she'd visited after Dad's death. That it tattered due to my envy was something I'd always thought could be repaired when she returned to the States. She had planned to come back, but kept postponing her return worried her dogs would not survive the New York winters. She was photographing birds at dawn when the Palestinians accidently landed their boat where she was, instead of a beach closer to Tel Aviv. They asked her directions, shot her, and went on to hijack a bus, killing 35 Israelis. (The details came from the only surviving attacker glorified in Palestine on each anniversary of the hijacking. When he returned home some thirty years later, he was celebrated as a hero.)

At Gail's parents' apartment, my cousin Charles took me aside to tell me I was in her will. I didn't understand. A will? At our age? What could she have had? And why would she leave me anything? Then I remembered. The reason for her visit to the States. Turns out she'd been a trust fund baby who had assumed my Dad had enough to leave me well off; I'd assumed she was a struggling artist. She was upset with my Dad; I, by her success. And now, reconciliation was impossible.

My cousin Estelle could barely look at me throughout the first days of Shiva. I tried –for lack of a better expression—to make nice; she was having none of it, or me. Finally, on day three, after I asked some inane question in an attempt to make conversation, out it poured, her voice bitter, her face contorted in rage. "I will never get over the look on your face when you came to Gail's show. Never!"

I tried to explain what that winter had been like. How I had tried calling Gail, but she'd been too busy to see me. How long I'd been looking for a gallery without success. And yes I had been jealous, resentful—all the emotions she'd seen—and was truly sorry. Slowly the muscles in Estelle's face relaxed; her husband, Johnny, came over and gave me a hug. It would take a few more years before Estelle and I could fully connect. For my 50th birthday, she gave me a large framed piece of Gail's that I loved. It hung in a prominent place in my loft until the colors faded.

With the money Gail left, $15,000. I immediately cast three pieces in bronze for Estelle to choose from. She chose the smallest. Needing absolution I begged her to take a larger piece, but she refused telling me the money was not to be thrown away. Some of it went into savings, some to have my tubes tied—I was tired of being on the pill and didn't want or trust a condom. It proved to be an unnecessary surgery, because soon after my sex life dwindled down to practically non-existence. Yes there was the odd man who, when my horniness got the better of me, I bedded for a night. But by and large, I led a celibate life.

My 25th high school reunion loomed. One of my classmates, another Gail with whom I'd recently struck up a friendship, had the idea for everybody to meet at my loft for lunch. She thought it could be a way to show off my work and have a get-together before boarding the bus to Riverdale. But Janey, my on again off again friend, got there first. Lunch would be at her house. I abhorred the thought of meeting women whom I was certain had married, had children, and were successful in their own right while I had very little if anything to show for my labors. No gallery, no husband, no children—only the loft and my sculptures and now they wouldn't be visible to validate my existence. I focused on my wardrobe. If nothing else I would look like an artist. (I was not alone in this need to differentiate oneself from the non-artist. When I lived at Bond Street, I was invited to a party Rauschenberg threw for charity. Roy Lichtenstein came in the specified tuxedo jacket making certain to smudge his sleeve with paint.) For the reunion I donned jeans, a red flowing shirt and boots—at the time a highly unorthodox outfit for an all girls' high school reunion.

Janey's apartment was on 72nd Street, the same block as Mom's who I made walk me to the building. Afraid I'd let my guard down and make an idiot of myself, I decided to abstain from alcohol if offered. There were about twelve of us—all on our best behavior—the atmosphere stiff. As expected, other than Lou, Janey's husband, I was the only one in pants. Finally Janey called us to the table. She and Lou stationed themselves at the heads though Janey barely sat, jumping up constantly while she apologized for her maid not showing. Nothing was said, but from the looks exchanged we all thought her behavior a bit bizarre—clearly I was not the only one without a maid. An awkward silence pervaded until Lou suggested we go around the table and fill in the intervening years. I felt sick to my stomach. The first person to speak said she was divorced; the second as well, though now remarried, and so on. Feeling less a failure, I said I sculpt and asked Lou for a drink. At the end of the day, Gail maneuvered everyone back to my loft for pizza. The oohs and aahs worked like a balm.

Early on I'd heard it took ten years for an artist's work to coalesce. First, techniques had to be mastered, then the various methodologies absorbed, until finally the artist could toss them all away allowing his or her own style to emerge. By 1981 I'd hit my stride—my work now distinctive. A friend procured a show for me at a gallery in Southampton. True to the roller coaster ride I felt my life to be, anticipation of a breakthrough into the art world had me fantasizing success. There still existed a split between my knowing the value of my work and how I perceived myself. With the work finished and waiting to be transported to the gallery, once again I focused on what to wear. I ended up with an elaborate black gauzy dress Janey had found which looked like something Louise Nevelson would don. As the guests piled into the gallery in their all white Hampton's outfits, I wanted nothing more than to run and hide once again. The dress that was supposed to serve as camouflage, masking my lack of self-worth, ended up confirming my suspicions. I did not know how an artist dressed, ergo I wasn't one. (The friend, long passed, who had gotten me the show, had hired me to work in his restaurants, and taken me to meet deKooning, bought the one and only piece that sold.)

Southampton Show

No matter how much clay I threw at Pegot Waring's studio in L.A., I hadn't mastered the ceramicist's art. Once again I began to envision pieces that defied the clay's limitations. I needed an armature, but armatures are internal structures, and clay cannot be fired with metal inside. I decided to build them externally and make them an integral part of the work itself. Apex Technical School—which turned out plumbers, welders and electricians—was just around the corner and off I went, finding the person in charge to sign up for welding classes. The head of the school, a frustrated artist himself, thought it would be smarter (and safer) if I purchased the necessary equipment which he would show me how to use. Into the loft came an arc welder, oxy-acetylene tanks, and large metal sheets to cover the wood floor.

With Oxy-acetylene Torch in Hand

The steel needed for the pieces was expensive and once more I was rescued, this time by a man from high school. We'd met at the reunion where he'd expressed interest in seeing my work. He was brilliant, an avid collector, a collaborator with artists, extremely wealthy and idiosyncratic, as well as easily infuriating and easily infuriated. He came from a real estate family and had access to all kinds of materials. Within no time he had sheets of steel delivered to my loft with no strings attached. We were never an item, nor even one-night bed fellows. Still, the relationship was fraught: I wanted a benefactor, but refused to be beholden; he was the supreme caretaker. It took just one crazy conversation during which he accused me of speaking to him while I was on the john—not true—to do us in. (We would meet again at the 50th reunion, try to establish a new relationship—only to have it dissipate in an instant when I said I wasn't a Zionist and he became so furious he hung up the phone on me. Like most things in my life, nothing is truly all bad. Through him I met a woman who has become a dear friend and when he and I meet—accidentally on the street or in a restaurant—we are both more than polite if not almost friendly. We just know to keep it at one short conversation and let it go.)

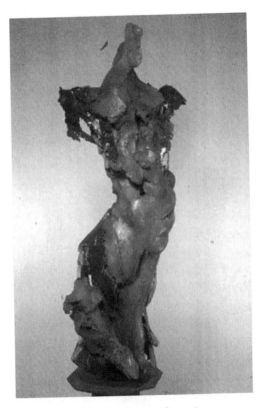

Man Terracotta/Steel

To separate the drawings from clay dust and metal grindings, I strung plastic across the loft one day managing to set it on fire. If it weren't for Pablo pawing at me—the welder's mask covering my face—we would have all been blown to bits. Panicked I could be evicted, I chose not to call 911 and somehow managed to put the fire out; I kept it a secret from everyone in the building. (I made the same choice when there was a fire on the second floor and I was on the street with my not-so-perfectly married high school classmate who had just arrived for a visit. We stood there with her suitcase and my two cats in their carry-all's deciding we'd only alert the firemen if the fire reached the fifth floor.)

I was wearing down both physically and mentally. I would sink into a depression, find a way to crawl out, and slide right back down again. Then the Loft Law was passed, the building sold and development begun. The six residential tenants formed a committee, hired a lawyer and made a pact not to let the developer pick us off one by one. The group appointed me liaison between them and our lawyer (to save on legal fees) paying me a stipend. Hanging over me was the threat of eviction, for even with a buy-out, most likely there'd be no place I could afford to go.

My German Years

A dealer called to say she had a potential buyer. Once again my hopes soared. They arrived. The dealer, normally outgoing and upbeat, appeared nervous; her client, a woman right out of a European movie—high cheek-boned, pale, thin, with long straight blond hair, and wrapped in a trench coat—clearly unsure of herself. The awkwardness of the two did not make sense until the dealer took me aside to tell me the woman was a Krupp and she hadn't been certain of how I'd react. Vera had already taught me to buy German goods, but a Krupp? They had made the ovens.

Before they left, the dealer's client, Christiane, invited me to a party the following week. I thanked her, took down the information and spent the intervening days doing battle with myself. If I went, I would be betraying "my" people." Forget the only times I'd entered a temple since my sister died was for a friend's parent's funeral, a cousin's bar mitzvah, and one trial balloon on Kol Nidre night during which I found myself uncontrollably sobbing. But on the other hand if I chose not to attend, I could be losing the chance to meet potential buyers. It was well known the Germans had started to collect art voraciously. Then again, I could be walking into enemy territory. Not that I'd ever directly experienced anti-Semitism—except once when I was sixteen and my High School singing teacher asked if I would sing at her church in Plainfield, New Jersey. She was their organist, so when a soloist took ill, she asked if I would step in. Despite my father's disapproval, I went. The choir and I donned our robes and when the time came filed into the chapel. I sat still in the pew replaying in my head the words of the Messiah I was to sing. Suddenly the minister's voice cut through.

"Go! Go out into the world, and convert the infidels, those who don't believe, and especially the Jews in all their depravity."

My teacher's hands fell upon the organ keys, the loud crashing sounds causing the entire congregation to jump out of their seats. I sat trying to figure out how I was immoral as I'd never even been kissed, while my teacher was having an affair with a married man. On cue and in a daze I got up and performed. The minute the service was over my teacher rushed over to me filled with apologies. I told her not to worry and walked over to the minister, my hand outstretched.

"Let me introduce myself. My name is Margo Krasne. That's spelled J-E-W-I-S-H and if you don't change your sermon, you will hear *Hatikvah* instead of Handel."

He changed the sermon.

Other than Irmgard, the governess who went with me to camp that first summer, the only other German I remember having met—as distinguished from someone of German Jewish heritage such as my brother-in-law—was a man my roommate Bobbi had fixed me up with for a double date. Bobbi's man, from Munich, was a tad oafish; mine, Aryan gorgeous, with a scar on his face as I'd seen in every war movie signifying all things Nazi. I couldn't contain myself.

"How did you get that scar?" I asked. "Fencing?" (I did not know then that while yes, the fencing facial scar was taken as a sign of manliness in the 19th and early 20th Centuries in Germany, German Jews also wore them proudly. That said, it was revived by the Nazis as a sign of German superiority.)

Whatever he said, and his words escape me if I even heard them, had me up in arms. Before I knew what had hit me I was yelling at him, demanding to know what he had done during the war. (Forget he was my age and could not have been more than 8 or 9 when it ended. Within seconds I was out of the restaurant—Bobbi trailing behind. Up to that moment, I hadn't even been aware of the anger I harbored against all things German.)

The possibility of a sale won out though I was never more aware of being Jewish as heading up to Christiane's party. Sort of how I felt when I first stepped out of a plane in St. Thomas, and as one of the few whites, viscerally understood what it felt to be "other." Christiane lived with her husband, a banker, in a rented Park Avenue apartment. It was white on white, both in décor and crowd. One woman appeared to be less reserved and more of the intellectual variety. Before the evening was out she invited me to her party the following week. I soon realized ex-Pats socialize often with those they might not find particularly their sort had they been back home.

Sylvie's party was far more interesting, filled with UN and embassy types as well as reporters from Der Spiegle, Die Zeit, as well as TV commentators from ARD and ZDF. Sylvie's husband Uli, an incredibly attractive man with a hard edge—in other words, my type—worked for the latter, and a young man named Rudiger worked for the former. It was Rudiger who came on to me. Aware I'd been turned on by Uli, I left with Rudiger. He was single, unencumbered and I needed sex.

Rudiger had a number of my father's tics. He couldn't sleep with sheets tucked in, he was overly fastidious about his clothes—laying everything neatly out before climbing into bed, and he was withholding as well as a tease. At 45, exhausted, frightened, broke, and desperate to be rescued, once again I began to clutch at straws. Hadn't my sister spotted her husband and known he was the one? Hadn't my mother married quickly after meeting my father? Even my brother proposed to a woman without really knowing more than she was pretty and came from money. Why not me? Rudiger was in New York for all of two weeks and I, in my heat and madness, assumed the affair would continue after he returned to Germany. I even told Mom about him, and the sheets, and she too managed to get swept away; by now she was 82 and frightened she could die and I wouldn't be able to take care of myself.

A week after Rudiger went back to Germany, there was a message from my doctor on the answering machine. It was the second time in my life I found my hands shaking so hard I couldn't dial the phone. When I finally managed to get the doctor on the line, it turned out I had precancerous cells. Of course, all I heard was the word cancer. I called Rudiger. I don't know what I expected. That he would rush stateside to hold my hand? That he would stay on the phone with me and tell me all would be all right? What I got was one shrug of a "So?" I was devastated. (I later learned that on his return to Germany he boasted to everyone he'd had an affair with a Jewess—but then I'd had one with a German as well, hadn't I?)

The next two years were a whirlwind of social interactions; potential buyers who didn't buy; German lessons at which I failed miserably—treating them like attacking a crossword rather than a language; and involvement with a couple's dissolution of a marriage. At every turn I was torn, fascinated by some of the intellectuals I met, learning how so many of the young Germans had gone to work on a kibbutz to atone for parental sins. I even became a friend of one of Germany's beloved newscasters whose father was a mayor of a small town and he, the son—a dyed in the wool liberal—was once a member of Hitler Youth. It was a roller coaster with no place to go but down as the stress and strain of trying to hold it all together took its toll.

On the night when a couple whom I had fully expected to buy a major piece, passed on it, I knew I was done. Except to move my pieces into a corner, I never put charcoal to paper or my hands in clay again. I turned down invitations to gallery openings and museum shows. They were all too painful—the same pain I'd experienced at the theater for years after deciding to quit.

Shoved to the Side

Mom and I were on the phone sometimes two even three times a day. I could feel her neediness even when it wasn't there. When she took a vacation, I packed her bags. When she needed to buy someone a gift, I shopped for her. When she didn't know how to fix her dinner, I directed her through it. And when she got sick, even though she had someone staying with her, I was up there, doing her nails, fixing her hair, resentful, but there. I longed for freedom. For the chance to be unencumbered, no longer bound by obligatory caretaking.

In 1983, her new doctor, whose own mother had just died and treated Mom as if she were his own, told us she could have a new valve and be as good as new and, if she chose not to, she'd have three years to live—just like that! Mom took the news seemingly unfazed. If someone had said that to me, I'd be in tears. Or shock. But Mom listened, nodded, and said, "No operation."

"Are you sure, Mrs. Krasne?"

"I'm sure. I'm tired of playing cards with the same women, listening to the same complaints, and I don't want to spend whatever time I have recouping in a hospital bed."

I remained quiet. No, "Please Mom, have the operation." No, "I need you." Yes, I felt like a shit, but the thought of seeing her through another surgery, running up to a hospital daily, then seeing her through recovery, depleted me. When she made me promise whatever happened, she would die at home. I promised. The countdown began.

I was still working as an extra and desperately trying to figure out what I would be if and when I ever grew up. One of the actors I worked with on a commercial mentioned that his wife worked for Money Magazine. "Why not talk to her? " I did and talked her into taking me on as a paper "girl." By now my thinking was more than skewed. I convinced myself that if I brought the reporters the mail, coffee—whatever was needed—I could learn their job by osmosis. I lasted all of two weeks and learned nothing—except, no one was going to hire me to write. Forget I didn't have the makings or the knowledge or anything else for that matter that went into being a reporter.

With nothing better to do with my time, I continued to write. Mom was having more trouble breathing. I had to give Pablo subcutaneous fluids daily. And my asthma was getting worse. Still, I wrote. Someone told me one of my classmates from the Playhouse was now an editor. I reached out and she offered to give her opinion on what I'd written. I sent her twenty pages. She went one better than the mother/daughter team who had decimated me before my first sculpture show."It's crap! Crap! Is that what you put down on a page? Toss it in the garbage. You'll never be able to write. Crap!" She went on in the same vein for what seemed like an hour but was probably all of ten minutes. Devastated, I called the person who had given me her name. He told me she was a lush and to take what she'd said with a grain of salt. But she wasn't wrong. Not really. I had been writing what was in my head. There was no thought of a reader. Or a plot line. Or description. As rough as she was on me, as hard as it was to hear, I learned a lot about what was lacking. And this time signed up for a class at the Y.

It was now the fall of 1985, two and a half years after the doctor's pronouncement. I was to meet Mom at B. Altman's to look at carpeting. She'd decided to spruce up her bedroom. An hour before I was to leave she called, frantic. "Where are you, you're supposed to be here, I couldn't find you." I told her we were not to meet for another hour. She got even more upset. I quickly dressed and raced to the store. I found her distraught. She kept apologizing for putting me out. Sorry she'd upset me. This wasn't my mom. Not the one I'd grown up with. Still, I refused to see what was before me. To believe the three years were almost up. For the next few months things appeared to return to normal. Except for Mom's breathing, I convinced myself she was doing well. The last photo I have of her was on her 85th birthday. She looked fabulous—at least ten years younger than her age. I would not allow myself to believe her memory wasn't as good as it had been. I was in total denial. She wasn't dying. Her mind was fine. She was fine.

Then came Passover. She'd begged off going to Marcia's. Said she didn't have the strength, so I said I'd bring the fixings to her. I found Mom completely disheveled, her robe hanging off her shoulder, her breasts exposed. She and the aide were giggling, playing a weird game. I put the food on the table, and sat, pretending we were having a Seder. Suddenly Mom started to stare at the chandelier that hung overhead clearly wanting me to look up as well.

"Do you know how you were conceived?" she giggled.

"How Mom," I said, frightened of the answer.

"Well, I'd just finished decorating the bedroom, and your father came home and got so excited, he wanted to have me right then and there. I begged him to stop, the wrong time of the month, but he wouldn't be turned away. See! I always told you, you were a love child!"

I finally understood the meaning of those words. I'd been the product of a rape. Granted one to which she acquiesced, but in my mind a rape nonetheless—sex and love interchangeable in my mother's mind.

A few weeks later I received a frantic call from her nurse to get up there fast! The door opened and there was my mother running around the apartment without a stitch of clothing. She was clutching her crotch and giggling as if she were a two year old who delighted in shocking the adults. The nurse and I corralled her. We held her tight while I called the doctor. He arranged for us to go to a facility that conducted brain scans. To this day I can't imagine what outcome he expected, or why I went along with it. Still, I got Mom dressed and into the elevator where she tried to climb on the elevator man. I held tight, frightened I would break her bones now so fragile. Once in a cab she kept trying to escape my arms, flinging herself through the window. At the facility I lay with her on the CT table, my body wrapped around hers so she would remain still long enough for the scan to take place. She was now clearly panicked as to what was happening to her and began to recite jumbled nursery rhymes. "Baa baa farmer in the dell sheep one two buckle my A B C D ..." Her eyes pleaded with me to tell her all would be okay. Somewhere inside, she knew she was losing her mind. The neurologist emerged from his office with the scan's results and, in front of Mom, as if she no longer existed, announced,

"It's dementia. The TIA's have shrunk her brain."

I wanted to kill him. He gave me a prescription for Haldol and sent us home. The Haldol calmed Mom into a state of non-existence. Aphasia it's called. My brother, in his inimitable way of avoiding pain, couldn't understand why I continued to go every day to be with her.

"She's got nurses around the clock. Doesn't even know you're there."

But I knew he was wrong. Knew, in spite of the Haldol, I could read her needs, whereas the nurses couldn't. My brother and his wife made a perfunctory visit. I dressed Mom and brought her into the living room. My cousin Estelle was also there. Making conversation, my cousin said the silver bowl on the table had been a wedding gift Mom had bought from her. Mom's voice shook my brother out of his denial. "Estelle's initials are on the bottom." Then she disappeared into herself again.

On Mother's Day, Mom had another stroke and fell on the bathroom floor. I called 911, her doctor was nowhere to be found; my brother out of reach on a golf course. The EMTs arrived. They wanted to take her to the hospital. I refused. I had promised Mom she'd die at home in her own bed. The EMT's called me a murderer and left with Mom still on the floor. Somehow the nurse and I got her into bed. A short time later, miraculously, she woke up as if nothing had happened. In fact she was totally present. We opened her Mother's Day gifts and, in typical fashion, she wanted to send them back. I made her keep the robe my brother's wife had bought. She put it on. Chatted with me about a new skirt I had bought. Then just as I was about to leave the room she off-hand-edly said, "Mildred Dreitzer told me one day I'd be grateful I had you." It hurt for but a minute. Then I took it for how she meant it: as a thank you.

It was getting too hard to run back and forth between the loft and her apartment. Not trusting the nurses, I moved in to be with her, cats and all. Pablo was hanging in, though he now needed flu-ids twice daily. What I didn't think to do was remove the little bit of jewelry from her room as it never occurred to me that nurses steal. On Friday evening, May 4th, Mom waved off the applesauce I was holding near her lips. She allowed me to apply Vaseline, then, she said, "No more!" and clamped her lips shut. I told her I would love her forever. She repeated, "Forever," and closed her eyes.

On Tuesday, June 6th, Mom lay in her bed gaunt to the point of emaciation. The nurse had told me to stay out of the room. She said my presence would make it harder for Mom to leave. Like an idiot, I believed her. The reality: she was pocketing Mom's jewelry. There wasn't much. But what there was I had wanted: three thin rings I had planned to wear in remembrance. At my request Chuck had come to the house. He hated being there—called it a "death watch." I couldn't imagine where else we should be. He talked about selling everything. I said there were things I wanted.

"Like that lamp." I said pointing to a black and bronze lamp that sat on a side table.

"You haven't had it up to now, so why do you need it?"

"But I did have it; every time I came up here."

Then the nurse came out. Mom was gone.

Chuck and I rocked between battles and hugs. He wanted a small funeral; I, a large one. Marcia pointed out Chuck had as much right as I to make a decision.

"But he hasn't been here to help," I cried. I was furious.

And Marcia, in her rational way, countered, "What if he lived elsewhere and had just come home? It was his mother as well."

I was in no mood for reason. Besides, why should his vote have held more weight than mine? Because my brother-in-law took his side? She wasn't his mother.

Chuck and Buddy booked a small room at Campbell's. I fumed. Then, on the day of the funeral, I walked in to find we were being moved to their largest room. So many mourners had arrived. I gloated.

With one month to go on Mom's lease, I remained in her apartment while having the floors in the loft Polyurethaned. I was hoping I could sell the loft for more than the developers wanted to pay to buy me out. I slept in the bed in which she passed, but not the one where she normally slept. I could not get the last image of her out of my mind. The bulging eyes. The skeletal face. The body no longer recognizable. It was not until a few weeks later, depression now leading me to afternoon naps—that I dreamt Mom appeared. She was propped up in bed, in the new white bathrobe, much as she'd been on Mother's Day. Only now she was her old healthy self. She had her hair coifed, her makeup on and she was looking straight at me. "Wait!" she said, her hand raised. "Wait!" I knew what it meant. "Take your time, lady. Stop rushing. You do things way too fast."

Not only did my brother not want to keep any of mother's belongings; he wanted to wring every penny he could from them. He was frightened. Thought the government was coming after him. He had won a lot of money in Vegas and hadn't reported his winnings. There is madness when someone dies and we were no exception. It took William Doyle, the head of the auction house, to save us from ourselves. He came to the house and, much like a marriage counselor, worked out a plan. He would write down the value of each item. Then we would take turns picking what we wanted. At the end, whoever's stash monetarily was higher, would pay the other the difference. My brother thought my niece and nephew should pay as well. As they hadn't been mentioned in the will, I wanted them to take whatever they wanted. I made a huge mistake. I should have simply put whatever my niece and nephew wanted on my list and be done with it—my nephew blamed me for a number of years for his having to pay anything. My brother, who had first said he hadn't wanted a thing, had his wife stand in for him. She craved plenty: every silver tray; every serving spoon. I was okay with most of it until we got to the silver grape scissors. My finishing touch on my mother's center pieces when I was a child.

"You don't need them," my brother's wife said. "You live in a loft. What do you need silver for?"

I went ballistic. "They are from my childhood. They are mine. It's you who don't need them for God's sake!"

Mr. Doyle brought her a beautiful pair (worth all of $25.00.) Mine stayed in my possession. As I said, there is madness when someone dies. I returned to the loft. To my chair. To staring out the window.

Part III

Rebirths and Deaths

January 1988

Susanne found her way into most of my conversations. It was more than just, "My therapist says …" It was more like, "On my way to Susanne's …" or "I was telling Susanne that …" or "Susanne thought the reason for …" But with it all, there was no progress as to who or what I'd be when I grew up. I felt time slipping by. Soon I'd have to leave the loft, but go where, and do what? Susanne suggested I see a career consultant. She even had a recommendation:

"She's just gone out on her own so the price will be reasonable."

I immediately suspected the woman to be one of Susanne's patients. More out of curiosity than any sense she could be of help, I went. I was a total snob condemning her because she worked out of her apartment—modestly furnished—on the Upper Westside. It didn't help that everything she offered up, I'd heard before. "You could try sales or decorating—you have an eye."

Back at Susanne's I was more than dismissive. "So, is she a patient?" I demanded. All I got back was the practiced blank stare of shrinks. I swear they teach those in school.

My calendars, now a series of books similar to Susanne's, offer up little as to what I did all day. There are jottings I know to be my appointments with her, friends' names presumably for lunch, dinner, or a movie, and a few "bldg"s most likely referring to meetings with our lawyer or the group—though I can't find the entry that informs when I actually closed on the loft. I know it had to be after October '87, because the week before the Black Monday crash I'd invested $5000.with a friend joking that my investments usually fail. Sure enough the money was gone in a day, but he was incredibly generous and reimbursed me. At some point I forked over $150k of my inheritance to buy the loft. My memory tells me it was Spring '88, but I have no way of proving this.

I remained in a holding pattern. Then one day in February, I put the key in my door as the phone rang. "Yes?" I answered, my voice sounding as if the call itself was the annoyance—which couldn't have been further from the truth. I have always preferred the phone over most means of communication—never fully understanding why I have to make a date for lunch or dinner with a friend when we've just spent an hour catching up on a call.

"What's wrong?" asked my friend on the other end.

"Sorry. I just wish I could teach those young things at the grocery store to say, 'Ask' instead of 'Aks' along with 'Please' and 'Thank you.'"

And my friend, a marketing maven, told me companies didn't pay to train at that level, but they did pay to train. I had no idea what she was talking about. This, even though a few years before, along with being a runner at Money Magazine for two weeks, I'd talked my way into writing a training manual for Xerox not having a clue as to what it was and what they wanted. They didn't ask for a second.

"Why don't you get Dorothy Sarnoff's book Never Be Nervous Again?" my friend said. "There are ads for it in all the papers."

And repeating my race for the Kathe Kollwitz monograph and the Kohut book, the moment we hung up, I ran the two blocks to Barnes and Noble. Within no time I was back home flipping through its pages, eyes popping. Tell someone to stand up straight and walk across the stage with confidence? I could do that! Have them speak out? I certainly know how to do that! I did a helluva lot more when I was at the agency directing actors in commercials. And the topper: Fix a client's tie? Who the hell couldn't do that? Without pausing to think, I dashed off a note to Sarnoff: "Dear Ms. Sarnoff. Loved your book! May I come work for you?" Seriously! No curriculum vitae, no discussion of what I could bring to the party. Clearly I was the supreme embodiment of Susanne's grandiose/narcissistic personality, but did I see it? No! I assumed Sarnoff would hire me on the spot. When all I got back was a hand-written note: 'Thank you, but we only take people who have trained thousands of executives'—lovely in retrospect, but certainly not enough for me at the time—I became highly indignant and sent off another missive telling her I'd directed hundreds of talent and non-talent—listing the well-known names—and when no response came, I said "Screw her!" and decided to open my own business.

I asked everyone for advice. Someone suggested I speak with a neighbor, a consultant, who might provide some ideas. I had been so myopically in my own world, I wasn't even sure what a consultant did, but gave him a call. He suggested I reach out to companies that put on corporate shows—at least I could learn and get paid at the same time. (One did eventually hire me to work with one of their speakers and while they said they liked what I'd done, they didn't hire me back.) Ever trying to be helpful, the friend who had suggested the Sarnoff book, arranged for me to meet with a friend of hers—a media coach.

The apartment was all beige. Walls, carpet, sofa, chairs: Beige! The media coach: grey. Grey sweater—cashmere, grey wool slacks, thin grey leather belt, grey suede shoes. I felt like a *schlub* in a long black skirt, a non-descript black sweater, covered by a slightly worn black coat. At least, her husband, a TV director, had on jeans and sneakers—black and scuffed. I focused on them for reassurance. The couple had a complete video set-up: lights, tripods, cameras, video playback. I couldn't imagine investing in all that equipment, nevertheless learning how to run it. I hadn't come prepared with questions—didn't know what to ask. They were very kind—their expressions verging on pity. I left and called Susanne from a street phone (we had them then.) "I can't be like that. She has the market cornered! I'm a failure."

My phone calls had to drive Susanne crazy. I know now they drove her patients mad. In my defense, Susanne never told me not to call. And she did take calls from other patients in my sessions. As for the perfect lady in grey, when I told my marketing maven friend how defeated I'd felt, she told me the apartment before the beige one was even more bohemian than mine. Fortified by my friend's reassurances, Susanne's foot in my back, and a Ritalin pill, I started looking for people to act as guinea pigs. The first woman who came, a friend of a friend, reminded me we had known each other when we were younger. I tried desperately to remember, but kept drawing a blank.

"We were at P.S. 6 together. "

"I remember so little of my years there," I told her.

"The girls had to take cooking and sewing classes."

"Prunes!" I said, "Stewed prunes! Over and over."

"Right. And sewing classes with the checked gingham." Then she fell strangely silent.

"What?" I asked.

"I poked a classmate's eye out."

And it all rushed back: my back to a wall holding up a piece of fabric while a classmate pinned a pattern onto it, the fear the pin would hurt me, running out of the room screaming, then so ashamed, I lied and said the pin had pricked my eye.

"You didn't poke anyone's eye out," I said and apologized more than once for all the guilt I had to have caused her all those years.

Another friend introduced me to a PR gal whom he thought could benefit from the way she presented herself. I can only hope she had a shrink of her own, because in my desire to prove I knew what I was doing—which in my mind was to 'fix her'—I treated her as if she were a lump of clay—something, rather than someone to mold. I told her she needed to wear scarves to cover her neck which looked old, said she should change her makeup, and to smile. I demoralized her to the point of justifiable rage.

I was like an octopus putting out feelers wherever I could. I decided I'd call the business "Speak Up!" My accountant—who came to me through Susanne—suggested I make certain no one else had the same name. So, in Rube Goldberg New Yorker Magazine cover fashion, I checked the Manhattan telephone directory and when the name wasn't there, figured I was in the clear. Four months, later I got a Cease and Desist notice along with a letter threatening a law suit. My lawyer explained that by adding my name to the title, I could make it legally mine. I only relay this to show how totally lacking in business savvy I was.

On April 18th, at my niece's wedding, I handed out business cards and announced I was going to coach people on presentation skills. I received polite but disbelieving stares. A few weeks later, trying to fill time, it dawned on me my clients—still basically non-existent, would need an audience. "People" I could place around the loft. Concerned I'd be wasting money by purchasing materials, of course I called Susanne for the okay and once received spent a full week drawing faces on muslin, attaching them to sticks secured onto wood bases, then draping them with costume jewelry—some of it mother's—along with ties, hats, anything that would give them individual panache—each one unique to itself.

On Memorial Day weekend 1988 I sent out letters selling my

services. That I still didn't quite know what my services were did not stop me. I decided as I had more of an affinity to those in advertising, I'd look in the Yellow Pages for names of agencies. The first letters went to agencies within a ten block radius and then I'd follow up with calls trying to secure an appointment with whoever was in charge. When the first round didn't produce any results, I extended the range to twenty blocks, then thirty, and so on. The letter opened with "Would you attend the theater if the Actors hadn't rehearsed?" It became my mantra for the first few years.

My father's, "if you need to study you are nothing" had never fully left my psyche, so when Susanne suggested I take a Public Speaking class to see what others were doing, my heart sank. Nevertheless, I followed orders and signed up for a one-day seminar at The New School for Social Research in Manhattan. The teacher had worked at a major company as head of training for ten years and was a published author. Once again I assumed she had the market cornered. Still, on a Saturday morning in June, I walked to the New School trembling. No different than when I headed up the block to my high school reunion—only this time there was no mother to walk with me—only Susanne's voice in my head from my early morning call: "You'll be fine. Go!" The classroom was large with chairs along three walls; the teacher—short, fiftyish and extremely uptight—busied herself setting up a slide projector. There had to be at least twenty-five of us. She started by asking we each state our name, occupation and why we were there. I sat along the back wall and as my turn neared I could feel panic rise in my throat and my face become flushed. By the time the person next to me finished, I could barely get out my name, nevertheless "I'm thinking of teaching communication." I kept my eyes to the floor imagining eyebrows raised around me.

The class turned out to be a dud; a textbook history of communication in slides starting with apes. Having regained a semblance of self, or perhaps acquiring a case of schadenfreude, I made eye contact with a young man who was seated against the wall to my left and a woman opposite him. The three of us became a diabolical trio—our eyes telegraphing mutual astonishment at the junior high school level of the content. We met up at the break and when he begged off, Lisa and I went to lunch together. Turned out she was, and is, an anesthesiologist at a major hospital here in the city who had been asked to lecture doctors around the country on a new device. Over lunch, after we ripped the class to shreds, I told her of my plans. When I mentioned I'd been contemplating holding a workshop, she not only said she would come, but said she'd bring a friend. I asked if she thought I should charge and if so, would $40 per person be ok. She thought it more than reasonable. I felt a spark of hope for the first time in ages.

Purely out of curiosity, we returned for the afternoon session. The teacher had set up a camera and we were to stand in front and say a few words. When she played mine back, I looked nothing like I imagined myself to be. Everything from my wardrobe to my facial expression seemed artsy-crafty—certainly not what I believed a presentation coach should look like. Clearly, I needed an overhaul. That said, the day did result in three positives: 1) I learned from Susanne that my panic attack came out of my grandiosity, i.e., I had to be better than everyone which is why I couldn't simply just state my name and be done with it. 2) I resolved not to use videos in my own workshops—too self-conscious making; and 3) I had a real client and a date for my first workshop: Saturday, July 18th, 1988.

I decided eight would be a reasonable number of participants. As I already had two, I only needed six more. A woman I'd struck up a conversation with at the next table at a restaurant—as I said everyone I saw was a potential client—agreed to attend, as did another who had been helping me design a flyer for the business. She too offered to bring a friend. Another woman signed up with her husband and the eighth was a woman whom I'm ashamed to admit became a wonderful client, but how we met escapes me.

It was not until a week before the workshop that it hit me: I had absolutely no content. I'd spent most of my time hunting for people and obsessing about what to wear and serve. Panicked, I called Dorothy who loved playing devil's advocate. As such, she was the perfect sounding board to help me formulate a structure. My starting point: an exercise that introduced the participants to each other, but would not require them to begin by announcing who they were and why they were there. It took a few hours of hashing, and finally I developed one in which each participant needed to inquire about the others without ever asking a question. It would get refined over time, but remained the opening of all the workshops held in my loft for years to come; one that taught the beginnings of eye contact, body language, and allowed me to take note of what aspect of each person's personal presentation of self needed to be addressed. The rest of the content for that first workshop came from the attendees and what they wanted to work on.

The workshop went well and everyone promised to recommend me to others. I scoured the streets to fill up the next one, starting conversations with anyone who looked like a young professional—on a bus, the supermarket, or the subway. I was much like the man in the old Borscht Belt joke who, walking along with a friend, asks each woman he passes, "Wanna fuck?" only to be slapped in the face every time. When his friend asks what he's doing, he answers, "It only takes one!" I found my one waiting for the number 6 train which happily was late in arriving. She was thirtyish, dressed in a tan suit, stockings, heels, and carrying a briefcase. I began with the typical New Yorker's complaint about trains not coming on time, she responded saying she was late for an appointment, and as the train neared the station, I inquired as to what she did. In order for her to answer, we had to sit together. When she said she was in Public Relations I told her about my workshop and she said she had two clients who could use some help. Most amazingly, she sent them.

I jumped at whatever lead was presented to me. "There's the Women's City Club—they might have women in need of your services … " A week later I joined. "Burson Marsteller is around the corner from you, it's a PR company, they probably use trainers" …. Next day I was on the phone making an appointment. Simultaneous to accosting strangers on the street, my days were spent cleaning the loft as if anyone who entered would notice the tiniest bit of dust. No matter how many times Susanne tried to make me understand that clients coming to me would have their eyes only on themselves, I kept cleaning.

Finally, my incessant phone calls paid off. I secured a meeting with the head account person at a small agency. The weather changed on the morning of my appointment and I arrived wearing my one and only outfit bought for summer use with goosebumps showing. I offered to give a half-hour talk on presenting for free. He agreed and a few weeks later I stood in front of a group of twenty-five fielding questions about how to get over nerves before a presentation, how to make a strong impression, how to deal with difficult clients. I don't think I had ever been as focused on what I was doing, memorizing faces and what they said as we interacted. I'd jotted down where everyone sat before we started so that after, when I met with the man who'd brought me in, I could give him feedback on each person's skillset and willingness to learn. I made certain to say the agency shouldn't waste its money on those who were averse to change. With great relief I nailed it—not off, according to the client, on one assessment. These free interactive sessions became a powerful selling tool for the first few years.

I was flying by the seat of my pants. When an agency president said he needed a coach for a pitch, I jumped at the chance. That I had never been part of a pitch—wasn't even sure I knew what one was—made no difference. I would learn on the spot. I can't remember if we won the business, but I know that a number of the people in the pitch became clients and advocates from that point on. (It didn't hurt that I came cheap.)

As my client list expanded, I realized I needed marketing materials. The first was basically a flyer that an upstairs neighbor, an art photographer who made his living as a graphic designer, helped me design. When it no longer sufficed, I began work on a brochure. I made a list of people to show each iteration—every suggestion incorporated before I passed it on to the next. I saved what I believed to be my final version for a copywriter whom I highly respected. On the day of a particularly successful workshop I could hear the fax (the old kind with thermal paper) clicking away. The minute the last participant was out the door, I raced over to retrieve it expecting raves. It read: Passive verbs suck!—the one four letter word I found particularly repulsive. Once again the roller coaster crashed but this time I didn't stay long at the bottom. Two more revisions and I got it done.

In November '88, The New York Times published a piece by Daniel Goleman—at the time the Times' science writer. It was all about narcissism and its off-shoot, grandiosity. It was succinct, insightful and clearly differentiated the differences between healthy and unhealthy narcissism. I read it over and over looking to see if Susanne had knocked the worst out of me.

A Shortened Version of Goleman's Explanation of Narcissism

Healthy: Appreciates praise—does not live for it.

Unhealthy: Has an insatiable craving for adulation; needs praise to feel momentarily good about self. (I no longer needed adulation, but certainly reassurance.)

Healthy: May be hurt by criticism, but the feeling passes.

Unhealthy: Is enraged or crushed by criticism and broods for long periods about it. (My brooding periods were shorter.)

Healthy: Feels unhappy, but not worthless after a failure.

Unhealthy: Failure sets off feelings of shame and worthlessness. (At the time, thought I had this licked. I'd be proven wrong.)

Healthy: Feels "special" or especially talented to a degree.

Unhealthy: Feels far superior to everyone else and demands recognition for that superiority. (No, to the latter, but then I kept myself out of competitive situations where reality could strike.)

Healthy: Feels good about himself, even if others criticize.

Unhealthy: Requires continual bolstering from others to have a sense of well-being. (Less of the continuum, but not totally gone.)

Healthy: Takes life's setbacks in stride though may be put off balance for a time.

Unhealthy: Reacts to the hurts and injuries of life with depression or rage. (Sometimes indignation—a la the Sarnoff letter. And depression yes, but thankfully never rage or I would have stormed out of therapy.)

Healthy: Does not feel hurt if no special treatment is given.

Unhealthy: Feels entitled to special treatment—ordinary rules do not apply. (This was never me, thank God!)

Healthy: Is sensitive to the feelings of others.

Unhealthy: Is exploitive and insensitive to what others need or feel. (By now I had begun to develop an understanding of other people's reality though it still took work.)

Susanne had become not only my therapist but also my mentor and teacher, explaining the difference between shyness and self-conscious behavior; the impact of shame; the fragility and explosive nature of what I was dealing with when I critiqued a person's persona. She had me reading book after book on psychology—my own collection now filling my shelves. Although I found much of the language impenetrable, I persevered with a dictionary of psychological terms handy at all times. (As a total aside: one of the most entertaining descriptions of why so much academic prose is so convoluted, was in the NY Times October 31st, 1993,entitled: Dancing with Professors, by Patricia Nelson Limerick. Her hypothesis: because no one ever asked the nerdy types to dance, they developed their own language in order to feel superior.)

By the end of December, over fifty people had come through my door. In January 1990 Susanne said she had a client for me. I tried to contain my excitement so I wouldn't appear grandiose, but the truth was I felt important and special. Then I remembered she'd sent me to the career consultant whom I had found wanting. It took weeks before her patient called, but when she did, her fears of speaking in public were intense and she ended calling me almost as much as I called Susanne. By March I had a client to send to Susanne. While I had already been on one of my evangelical streaks—I had brought Dr. B plenty of patients and now talked up Susanne to anyone who would listen—this would be the first time I could recommend someone who was not a friend. She asked the client for permission to share with me pertinent information; he acquiesced. And while she managed not to give away anything of a truly personal nature, she did inform me I was dealing with a passive/aggressive personality. It would be the start of a treacherous tightrope Susanne and I would walk—not always well.

I began to up my prices in small increments. I also limited the workshop size to a maximum of five; decided participants would benefit from not knowing each other—a safer environment in which to expose weaknesses—and succeeded in making my life more difficult. Try getting five people from five different companies together on the same day. Still, my reputation built and the roster of company names on my client list ranged from AMEX to Young & Rubicam Advertising to Planned Parenthood of NY to Good Housekeeping. It all amazed me. It certainly amazed Susanne.

"I showed off your brochure to my group," she said one day, proudly holding up her copy. "I must tell you, I have never worked so hard and so furiously as I did with you. So little time and you without any marketable skills."

My first reaction was to be thrilled—that my success was a source of her pride. At the same time, I was taken aback that she hadn't seen my potential. But so little time? If she'd been so worried, why hadn't she arranged to work with me even for a day during her time off? Still, I brushed those last thoughts aside and allowed the good-enough-mother to burst with pride at "our" accomplishments. Of course, she couldn't quite leave it at that.

"You took your worst trait and turned it into a business."

I roared knowing exactly what she meant—would repeat it often to friends. I had taken my need to fix things, to have everything just right, and put it to good use. Unstated was the fact she was also implying that I could be quite critical. My Book of Shoulds she called it. But then, we do pass on to others what was done to us. Dad's constant need for perfection in his women got turned into my need to "fix" others—not to mention myself.

A Momentary Setback

To say I lived in a constant state of anxiety doesn't come close to my reality. I was up and dressed at the crack of dawn, champing at the bit to hit the phones. I never left the house without looking totally put together—what if I ran into a client? I had turned into someone my mother would have appreciated. Dressed, coifed and made up! Then came a day when two jobs came in: one was to hold a seminar for Barnes and Noble down south; the other, to speak in front of 200 professional women at their dinner. I was off the charts with excitement. Nothing was going to stop me from going, not even a diagnosis of colon cancer.

I received the news following a ridiculously long battle with a gastroenterologist who, after doing a lower endoscopy (this before Katie Couric's TV colonoscopy,) swore that I was perfectly healthy, just a Type A woman. In other words: a hysteric. When I didn't relent that something was wrong, he threw up his hands and agreed to my having a barium enema while he was off on vacation. I might have had a smug moment of vindication when he returned, but it came after the Indian radiologist's pallor turn a ghostly green upon seeing a malignant tumor in the transverse colon on the screen—something not reached by an endoscopy.

Of course, the gastro guy ran for the hills, and a surgeon took over setting an immediate date for the tumor's removal. To say I was in denial is putting it mildly. As I was more afraid of losing my business than dying of cancer, I begged the surgeon to delay the surgery so I could handle both engagements. In retrospect, if I were dead there'd be no business, but on the other hand, if I didn't have a business … We compromised: I'd give up B&N which was two weeks off and out-of-town–they were very kind and sent a huge bouquet of flowers—and he would allow me a three day extension so I could give the talk in New York. Did I mention it was in the middle of February? And because I'd broken my big toe I had to wear ugly open shoes even in the snow? No matter. The day of the talk, I underwent the obligatory pre-surgery CAT scan and was home putting on my makeup when the surgeon called.

"We saw a spot on your liver and I need you to have another scan tomorrow."

All the previous weeks of denial dissolved. The tears flowed as

I put on, took off, put on, took off my makeup until, eventually, I managed to get myself under control. Luckily, the talk was close by at the National Art's Club. So, blocking out the possibility I was dying, I gimped over, entered the club, and was escorted into a ballroom filled with at least twenty-five round tables—all beautifully set ready for the guests, and a hors d'ouevres table clearly meant to welcome all. Except that other than me and the waiters, there was no 'all'. We were the only ones there. Now I'm known for arriving early—sometimes to the consternation of my hosts—but this was crazy. The waiters stared at me, I at them, and the minutes went by—at least twenty.

Eventually a slightly overweight, grey haired lady marched in followed by nine or ten other women. She walked right over to me, introduced herself as the head of the organization and with a rather bland apology explained that the woman who was to have sent out the invitations had a drinking problem and had forgotten to do so. I assumed she'd cancel the evening and send us on our way, but no! Not only would we "carry on"—her words—but we would sit at the dais, as planned, facing out onto an empty room. I desperately wanted to scream, "For God's sake, I might be dying and this is nuts!" Then "our" leader announced that as long as they were paying me an honorarium—she left out the word measly—I should get up and give my talk. As I stood in front of the dais, my back to the empty tables, I kept thinking about the Mary Tyler Moore episode in which Ted decides to open a school, rents a hall, and convinces Mary et al to be on his Board. Only one student shows. He sits in the audience—Ted's "Board" on stage—and demands his money's worth. By the time I sat down I couldn't contain myself and whispered my diagnosis to the woman on my left. She, meaning well, told everyone else. There was a tremendous amount of "There, there" "You'll be fine" and "Don't you worry now" until one woman—with steely eyes, jagged bones, and tightly pulled back black hair, a retired Air Force Colonel, proclaimed that she had breast cancer and was refusing surgery and if I had a brain in my head I would do the same. "So what if you die, we all will eventually." The evening broke up shortly thereafter. Obviously I survived. Whether the colonel did, I have no idea.

Chuck flew up from Florida to be with me. Our dead sister's specter hung over us as we waited for me to be wheeled down to the OR.

"Will you stay until it's over?" I asked knowing how he dreaded hospitals.

"Not leaving."

"Promise?"

"Promise." His eyes welled up and, as if on cue, so did mine.

I woke up in a haze. I could make out Marcia, Chuck, the surgeon, and even my regular doctor in the doorway.

"You're going to be okay. They got it all," someone said.

Luckily there were no nodes involved. No chemo. Just a number of vain attempts to put back the fourteen pounds I'd lost in the process with friends feeding me mashed potatoes. (The following year my writer friend Anna would die from a surgical complication related to her colon, colon cancer would also take the life of a friend from Doyle Dane days, and another friend would announce he too had the diagnosis, "Weren't you one of the lucky ones," he said. Two years later he too would be gone after a horrific battle.)

Unhealthy Narcissism Rears Its Head—Rightfully!

From early on I'd managed to get a number of speaking engagements and spent hours writing scripts each crafted for the specific audience: a group of young professional fund raisers; the NY Lawyers Association; Women in Radio and TV Advertising. Some of these went well, and I added to my client list; others, where I bombed taught me something I could pass on. (Mispronouncing 'cacophony' so it comes out 'cack-o-phony' does not attract clients.)

It was now 1993, I was invited to speak at Callan & Company's 20th Anniversary Conference in San Francisco at the Fairmont Hotel. A financial firm, they assigned the topic: Improve Your Portfolio Manager's Sales Skills. Reasonable enough if I knew what a Portfolio Manager did, but I hadn't the slightest idea—anything to do with the stock market escaped me. I called a few clients who gave me a crash course. It would not be enough. Then, right before I left, a well-meaning friend said, "If you make it at Callan, you've got it made." I imagined clients flocking to my doors. No more cold calls. No schlepping to various events to network. Life would be wonderful. Now, to be fair, besides my lack of knowledge of the industry, there were forces working against me over which I had no control: I'd been assigned an hour and a half slot (too long for any speaker) at 3:30 in the afternoon on the second day when the attendees were more than ready for the golf course; the audience was filled with Portfolio Managers who took umbrage having to listen to someone tell their marketing people how to improve their skills; the audio man, more used to pinning Lavalier mics onto men's' lapels, did not like what I was wearing and attached mine to Mom's silk scarf—worn to every event for luck; and last, they wanted me to stand at eye level with the audience rather than on a platform—ridiculous in front of 250 people. So besides my not knowing what the hell I was talking about and my voice disappearing as the microphone kept slipping away, to add to the debacle, one woman interrupted trying to prove she was far more knowledgeable than me, and a man walked out soon after I began, making certain everyone saw his exit. Now if I had been speaking on any other subject, I would just have gone down as a lousy speaker. But I was supposed to be the expert on presentations and clearly I couldn't give a decent one. The only thing I did right was to cut the talk short by almost an hour. It would take over five years for me to utter the word Callan without feeling as if I were being flayed alive.

A few months later, In Tucson, I stood in front of a similar audience at AIMSE the marketing association for the financial community. Many of the same people were there. One woman even came up to me the night before at the cocktail party, and with a huge smile said, "I saw you at Callan. Can't wait to see you pull those arrows out again." But this time I came prepared. I demanded a platform, made certain my microphone was attached to my lapel and stayed far away from anyone who could bring me down. When I took the "stage" the old performer in me emerged. I loved being there and the audience responded. It was as if I was back at the Nautilus belting out a song. Most of my financial clients can be traced to that particular engagement. Not that the memory of Callan didn't lurk in the background for quite a while, but eventually I started using the experience as a teaching tool with clients, and my skin grew back.

Agoraphobia and All That Jazz

I'd never been an intrepid traveler. Nor did I ever have even a smidgen of wanderlust. But now most of the jobs that came in put me on the road. Sometimes I went along the northeast corrido by train or car—always with a driver as I don't drive; more often by plane down south and to the Mid-West—each trip causing enormous anxiety. First, there were the cats. I admit to being a highly neurotic cat owner who could not leave my animals alone even for a night. (A year after I adopted Pablo, I'd brought in Miquel, then when he had to be put down, Bouche and so on—not counting Soc, there were six in all.) Was I playing out my own childhood fears of being left alone and transferring all of it onto the animals? Most likely. But days before each trip I'd check and recheck the arrangements, then pack and repack not to mention hound the cat sitter to make certain she or he would arrive on time. Amazingly, my panic would dissipate once I was downstairs and into whatever vehicle I'd ordered. The return trip was no better. Not until I turned onto my block and could see my building standing, did I actually begin to breathe normally. The advent of the cell phone helped, for as soon as we landed I'd dial Dorothy, or a friend in my building, anything that could let me know all was right in my world. Eventually the calls went to my brother who was now suffering with a complicated blood disorder—too many antibiotics and steroids when he'd contracted the staph infection after his open heart surgery. Strangely, I never called Susanne.

Susanne labelled me an agoraphobic in spite of the fact I had no fear of crowds or public spaces. I have spent much time researching the word and no where can I find her definition. But when Susanne declared something to be the "truth," you didn't argue. Her explanation revolved around the parent taking the child to school for the first time. "When a child becomes hysterical, she isn't worried about going to school, but whether or not the mother will be there when the school day is over. In your case, whether home would be there at the end of camp, at the end of the school day, or whether they'd return from one of their many trips. Your emotional home was never secure. It had nothing to do with your building being there, or even your mother being at home. It had to do with whether they really were there for you!"

"Got it!" I said, though something still nagged at me.

"Then what's bothering you?"

"My parents travelled all the time. Loved it."

"But you experienced their trips as abandonment. Certainly not pleasure." So, from then on I was an agoraphobic, the actual definition be damned.

More Blurring Of Boundaries

By now I had sent a number of clients to Susanne. I was like my father, who having brought home a fabulous melon or cheese wanted everyone to taste it. And Susanne was sending people to me. She was becoming more open in what she shared, sometimes shocking in her comments.

"Susanne, if he so frustrates you, why not send him on to another therapist? You can't be helping him if you're this angry."

"His last therapist committed suicide, I can't reject him." Then, with a laugh she added, "Probably, I would have jumped as well."

I knew boundaries had been crossed, but let's face it, the more I was included in the treatment of one of her patients, the more important I felt. That sense of importance only strengthened when some of my clients were then sent on, with my knowledge, to Dr. Mas, the psycho-pharmacologist. I began to see myself as part of a trinity. Susanne did nothing to dissuade me. In fact it was she who said, "You take care of the external; we the internal."

I kept hearing if I wanted to grow my business I needed PR. Each PR person I spoke with said I needed to write a book or there'd be nothing they could do for me. Fearful that a book would take over my life, I kept putting it off until someone said it would give me the credentials I needed. That did it! It would be my college thesis! And so I started in. Every page I wrote went with me to Susanne. She would read and correct, read and make suggestions, read and send me to buy another book on psychology. It was slow and arduous work not only stringing complete sentences together, but making them sound as if they came directly from me. It took months upon months for me to achieve any sense of clarity in thought or structure.

A friend of a friend had a literary agent who took me on, but had no luck in selling the concept to anyone. Then in April 1996, at a workshop for the Marketing Department at Warner Books, Karen Torres, one of the participants, commented that I should write a book. I wanted to hug her having vowed not to mention mine as I thought it totally unprofessional to do so. But when she opened the door, I told her I had one almost ready to go. She asked if I had an agent and when I said yes, she and Christine Barba, the department head, told me to have him contact them. And that was that. I would be a published author.

It took way too long, but at last the book went to the editor, back to me for some changes, and then out of my hands to wait for the final proof and the mock-up of the cover. It arrived the day my doctor ordered a chest X-ray—my breathing worse than normal. Turned out my lung had collapsed and I was ordered to call my doctor immediately. Instead I phoned my editor blaming her for the state of my lung. All right, maybe the lung had collapsed from asthma and pneumonia, but the cover could have been the final tool of its deflation. I mean an old fashioned radio mic on what was supposed to be a contemporary take on speaking in public? A title that used "Say It" rather than "Speak Up!" my business name? And the topper: my name misspelled! So it was only my middle initial, but I don't have a period after the T, and putting one in was the last straw. Only after I called my agent who said he would handle things, did I call my doctor who arranged for a hospital room and what turned out to be a three week stay. My agent fought as hard as he could, managing to get rid of the mic, but the period never got deleted. In the end, the editor got even; instead of a mic I got a different font for each word on the jacket all in different colors. It looked like it had been designed by someone on LSD. Still, I had a book and, with any luck, renown and royalties.

Weirdly, the collapsed lung and pneumonia caused me to panic in a way I hadn't with the cancer. Susanne said it was a delayed reaction. Whatever it was, death started to take center stage in my mind. We were now nearing 1997; the eleventh year my brother and I had referenced at Mom's unveiling. "Someone's going to die," I kept saying. I didn't believe it could be me even though, God knows, I'd had enough asthma attacks at three in the morning which could have caused my demise. No, I believed it would be Chuck. Susanne considered my fears insane.

"Yes he might die, but not because of a grave and an eleven year curse."

The tension was relieved when a client informed me they'd added my book to a package his agency was presenting to one of their clients, an airline. The concept: it would be in a gift bag for all business class clients. I couldn't believe it! Finally, a real break! Two weeks later he called to say they lost the client. Down I went again. Then my brother-in-law's testicular cancer reappeared. As he'd always played down his original diagnosis, I'd assumed it had been exorcised like mine. No such luck, in September, on the day of my book signing at Barnes & Noble, Marcia, my niece and nephew were at home waiting for the doctor's call and the test results. A client threw me a dinner at a restaurant to which Chuck came, but he spent most of the time racing to the phone to hear the verdict. Before dessert he returned with, "He has six months to a year." To say the joy was taken out of my "day" is an understatement.

Of course, Susanne gloated. "See! It won't be this year. Your brother appears to be doing better. Your brother-in-law has at least six months and by then we'll be in 1998. I told you, all magical thinking on your part."

One month later, Buddy died from a blood clot, a result of the chemo. Susanne went into shock when I called to tell her.

Separations

I started to call Susanne less and less. At first, I consciously stopped myself from dialing, but soon I realized the need was no longer there. I was still seeing her twice a week and suggested cutting down to once. I got the old "we'll see." Simultaneously, a Director of Human Resources, who was both client and friend, took me aside and advised against my bringing up any form of therapy in my private sessions with her people. It was okay to suggest Beta Blockers, but no matter how phobic the client, not a therapist. I agreed not to only with her clients, but my others as well. I was very proud of how far I'd come and waited for Susanne to notice. Instead, in the middle of a session, she shocked me with,

"You haven't sent anyone to me lately, is something wrong?" The look on my face must have telegraphed she'd gone too far. She quickly tried to backtrack. "I just was curious. Not that you should have, just wondered."

I didn't say anything. Couldn't, was too stunned. Almost the same as when a few years earlier I had brought up, admittedly for the umpteenth time, being tied to the table by Uncle Murray, and she had responded with, "Enough! You want to know from pain? I had to have my adenoids out without anesthesia!" Or when I had relayed the Passover story, and she'd exploded with, "Your mother wasn't raped! Mine was, by the Russians, on our kitchen table while I hid in the closet. Your mother had sex with your father! And since she giggled telling you, she enjoyed every damn minute!"

My 60th passed. I'd celebrated with three couples and Chuck at the Waldorf's Rainbow Room. I'd asked they pay their own way which they did willingly. In retrospect, I should have picked up the tab, but still lived as if I were a starving artist. I had visions that Chuck and I would take over the dance floor as in the old days. But between my asthma and his heart we could barely move. A few weeks later, over lunch, Chuck said, "You know, Buddy always said you wouldn't find a man until we're all dead."

I didn't state the obvious, that if that were the case, I only had one more death to go. Yet I couldn't help but wonder if it weren't true—that maybe the three men in my life who had been a constant presence—my brother, brother-in-law and Dad—had been a combination that no one man could compete with. Chuck the great dancer and bon vivant; Dad the disapproving arch-angel; and Buddy the man who made certain the family stayed together even after my sister died and he remarried. I mentioned his remark to Susanne, but she skipped over it just as she had when I came back from a trip having been attracted to one of my typical 'withholding' men. Sex rarely if ever found its way into our sessions.

In February of '99, when my travel schedule had become even heavier than usual, I called Susanne to change an appointment. Her voice sounded raspy, asthmatic. It scared the hell out of me.

"What's wrong?"

"Nothing."

"Susanne, for God's sake. You sound horrible."

"The painters are here. House filled with dust."

"Get the hell out of there, for God's sake. Go to a friend's. You shouldn't be there."

She told me in no uncertain terms to mind my own business. At our next session she bristled when I said she sounded asthmatic and should get it checked out. Then towards the end of April, for the first time in the thirteen years I'd been going to her, she called to say she had the flu and needed to cancel her appointments for the next week. She had never, ever missed or cancelled a session—no matter what. She had never postponed—never not answered her phone when in session. Yet when I called to see how she was feeling, I got an answering machine. Not once, but twice and then again. On May 4th, returning from a job in Connecticut, I stood on the platform of the train station trying to reach her leaving message after frantic message. Everything told me this was dire. When I got home there was a message from a voice I didn't know. I shouldn't worry. She was recouping at friends in New Jersey. Of course it was all a sham. She was in St. Vincent's Hospital and had her friends call from their cell so I'd see the New Jersey number— all to throw me off track.

A few weeks later she returned to work tethered to an oxygen tank and popping pills. It took two visits of prying for her to admit she had Stage 4 lung cancer with a year to live. It was all so surreal. I begged her to go to the country early. To take the time to care for herself. But no,

"I have things, must do. July 4. Will see in Fall."

There was nothing I could do, but go along with her. I certainly couldn't tell her now that I thought we should be terminating therapy. That I had thought so for quite a while. I would just have to play it out. I began to get calls from a number of patients I had sent to her, asking what was wrong. "She didn't come to the door." "She appeared out of it." All of it true. I told each what was happening and left them to make their own decisions about whether or not to continue to see her. The next few weeks were hell. Then the call came; she was in the hospital.

Another woman stood outside her room with me. We introduced ourselves. It would turn out she and her husband were Susanne's Jersey friends. Eventually I was told I could go in. I sat at the edge of her bed. She was curled up in a fetal position. I had no words and put my hand on her foot which was exposed. She jerked it away. I said good-bye and left. No tears. Just numb. For many of the thirteen years I had known her, whenever I would panic before one of her trips out of the country, or her insistence on driving out to the Hampton's in the middle of a snowstorm at night, she would assure me she would outlive us all. And now she was dying.

Here's where my calendars confuse. I have hospital written all over them, but whether it was to see Susanne or Chuck, who was in and out of one, I can't be certain. For the year after Buddy died, Chuck shuttled back and forth between Florida where he had stowed his wife and Marcia's where he camped out until she said it was time for him to find his own place. He did. A small furnished ugly apartment in Westchester where he'd placed a Do Not Resuscitate sign on the fridge. I felt sick when I visited.

I went once more to see Susanne listening from the hall to her argue with her niece. "I can walk home. I can. I don't want an ambulance." She sounded petulant, unreasonable and clearly not in control of her mind. I never saw her again.

Chuck needed constant infusions of blood. I felt guilty for him using up so much of the hospital's supply in his futile effort to stay alive. I went upstairs to offer my own. Years before the asthma, I had given blood every three months. Once on steroids, the donations were rejected. Now, temporarily steroid-free, I filled out the form. The nurse came out. "I'm sorry, but we can't take you. You've had cancer."

I went into a total melt down. "But that was eight years ago and I didn't have chemo, or radiation, or anything of the sort. All they did was snip it out. I'm fine!"

"Sorry," she repeated, "once a cancer patient, always a cancer patient!"

I made it back to my brother's room feeling side-swiped. I was still a cancer patient. I could still die. Another shock greeted me as I entered. The last of his mistresses sat near his bed. He's had a slew—one, he'd even brought to my loft at Bond Street while I went to take care of our Dad, and who had left him for a woman.

I adored the story. He who had accused me of being a lesbian had been screwing one. Her words to me when I talked with her later, "He kept thinking size was all that mattered." (Strange what we learn about our siblings.) Anyway, I knew this particular affair was over. As she would later say, "I married one alcoholic, I wasn't about to marry another." Over or not, she was still whom he turned to after Marcia. Once again I felt pushed out of the way which didn't stop me from taking the train to visit him almost daily.

I re-established contact with Regina who had first introduced me to Susanne. Now that my therapy had ended, there was no reason for us not to talk. She kept me abreast of what was going on at Perry Street, though she also let me know that she and Susanne had been estranged for some time. On July 29th the call came. Susanne was dead. I didn't cry. Couldn't. Then I got on the phone and called various patients of hers, both former and present, as well as my friends and family. Did I mention that Susanne had once accused me of never being able to separate on my own, but always relying on death to do it for me? Once again she was proven correct.

When Susanne lay dying, I wrote a piece on what it would be like to not have her waiting for us at the end of September. I thought of it as a perfect August op-ed piece for the NY Times. I sent it over to her brother who had taken care of her that last month. He called and asked that I make copies to hand out to the guests at the funeral. He also said I could join him in the car he'd hired to take us out to Amagansett where she was to be buried. On the morning of the funeral, as he and I walked back with coffee for the ride out, I mentioned how much Susanne hated her new neighbors and would turn over in her grave if they ended up buying her share of the building. He sounded like Chuck speaking of me, "My sister. She can be crazy." Yet he had left his life in Germany to be with her, just as Chuck had raced to my side. I was still looking for similarities between Susanne and me no matter how far-fetched.

There would be five of us in the car plus the driver: a couple, a psychiatrist and his wife from Boston with whom Susanne had become quite close on her sojourns to Vieques, Puerto Rico; a close female friend of hers, her brother and me. They all whispered amongst themselves. I felt like an outsider. Well I was. I was the only patient. When we arrived at the house, people had begun to gather. At some point we all headed up to the cemetery, everyone forming an enormous semi-circle. A few people chose to speak. Her friend from the car gave an over-the-top eulogy, personal and surprising. Were they lovers? Hard to tell. Another friend spoke briefly. Then her brother. It all felt cold in spite of her friend's emotional tirade. I felt compelled to speak for her patients. Her friend had addressed her talk to Susanne directly as if she were there. I mimicked her approach. Do I remember what I said? Absolutely not. But I do know I wanted those obvious Hampton's intellectual to know she had done great work.

Back at the house a number of people read my piece and commented on it. Regina pointed out the ex-lover to me—the one who had left Regina's husband's show just before Susanne had arrived all those years before. He appeared effeminate and weak, not at all what I had imagined. Another man, whom I found extremely attractive, began to make conversation, commenting on my essay. I immediately imagined that Susanne had arranged, from her perch wherever she was, to leave me in good hands. Then a woman, whom I judged, correctly, to be another shrink, came up to me.

"How do you think she handled her dying?" she demanded.

"Terribly," I said, surprised by the question and her tone.

"And why?"

It was obvious I was going to be interrogated. "Are you a therapist, as well?" I asked.

She nodded, yes, and just then the man I thought would be my next affair joined us. They were clearly a couple. "And what do you think she did wrong?" his wife continued, ignoring his presence.

"Her denial. Her seeing patients even though she couldn't breathe or think well."

"And how did her other patients handle it, do you know?"

"Not really." And then, in a most lighthearted manner, trying not to expose my own disappointment, "I thought the scientist in her would record her illness and when she couldn't write anymore would have me record it for her."

She didn't react with either surprise or humor. I couldn't help but wonder if she was scouting for patients for her own practice. (I would be proven wrong. For a period of time we became friends, though I always felt she saw me as a wounded bird whose wing needed fixing.)

Marcia, as pre-arranged, picked me up. She had rented a house in Amagansett, which she had done for many summers, and knowing I would be attending the funeral, invited me for the weekend. By this time she had started to see someone, but knew how important it was for me to have alone time with her. On Sunday, Chuck called. I was in the room. "And when did they say that?" Marcia asked in well-modulated tones. "I see." Pause. "And how do you feel about it?" Pause. "You don't have to do what they say. It's your choice." The conversation ended, she hung up the phone and turned to me. "They want him to go to hospice."

It was as if someone had picked up a loaded shotgun, took aim, fired and instead of the bullet felling me on the spot, it propelled me out of the house and into the empty streets. I don't know how long I walked until my body could calm down, but at some point it hit me, I have a lousy sense of direction. Without a cell phone to call Marcia, if I didn't head back, I'd be lost in no time. I found my way back. Chuck opted against hospice. Death too frightening for him to face.

I decided, along with Susanne's friends from New Jersey, to hold a memorial service for her patients. In cleaning out the house, her friends had found a list, but few addresses or phone numbers. I offered to look it over thinking there'd be a few I'd know. Another shotgun blast. Seventeen of the twenty one names who were currently seeing her had come through me. Without my 'shilling' for her, she'd have been down to four. So for all her accusations of my not being able to give up my role as family caretaker, I had turned into hers.

More shocks followed. "Of course she was gay," Regina said. "Well, she swung both ways. Often said, 'If you can't be with what you want, you take what's in front of you.'"

When I inquired why there weren't more laudatory remarks at the funeral. Great acclaims of friendship. Regina again, "She had alienated so many, argued with so many, I told you even I hadn't spoken with her in years."

But the strongest after shock came at listening to the anger expressed at the memorial service by those patients who either had not been able to separate from her or had to do it by waging war. Very few expressed sadness. Clearly, if she had lived, my leaving her would have been messy to say the least.

I poured myself into work and found solace by putting my feelings onto paper. I was no longer fearful that writing would take over. It was a sideline to my business. A few pieces became the basis for short stories, others were just rants. My brother continued to refuse hospice, but was now confined to a hospital bed with intravenous transfusions almost daily. The constant visits up to White Plains were wearing, but impossible for me not to make.

"What time is it?" he demands. Time has become a fixation.

"Six-twenty."

"They're late with dinner."

"*It should be here soon.*"

"*It should be here now,*" he roars in good old Strombolian fashion.

Maybe it means you're getting better. Certainly looks as if they're not as concerned."

My attempt to present him with other ways to deal with frustration goes unnoticed.

"*Go see where it is!*" he demands.

"*I'm sure it will be here in a moment,*" I tell him.

"*Go Goddamn it!*"

Which I do. I actually get up, walk to the door and of course run smack into the aide coming in with the tray.

And

"*Where're you going?*"

"*To heat up the soup I brought.*"

"*When I want soup, I'll ask.*"

And

"*I think I'll head home,*" I say.

"*No one asked you to stay.*"

"*If I leave now I can get the express train.*"

"*So go!*"

"*I'll be here in the morning.*"

"*You don't have to come at all.*"

"*Tomorrow morning,*" I repeat and pick up my coat as he tears into a roll. In a few seconds he will have indigestion. I don't bother to warn the nurses.

And

"... you've got to eat something."

The room erupts; each of his volcanic outbursts seemingly stronger than the last.

"I don't want to eat. I don't want to talk. I just want to be left alone. Do you understand? I don't want you here. I don't want anyone here. Do you hear me?"

"Everyone can hear you," I whisper, much the way one lowers one's voice to a child in the midst of a tantrum.

"Good. Then just sit there and say nothing!"

I wanted to roar at the absurdity of it all, but knew enough to just sit quietly. I kept hoping for some incredible insights on his part. Some change of behavior now that death was so near. Perhaps a reconciliation with his son. Something. But none came. He had one brief insight, more of a flicker than a light.

"Perhaps Mom shouldn't have had me skipped so often."

"Probably. Couldn't have been easy being the youngest of the group." I kept to myself that if perhaps he had been a slight child, short, frail, his buddies would have realized how young he was. But he was tall, good looking, and charismatic and they expected him to keep up with them.

"Forget it. You know the trouble with you?" he asked, putting any insight to an end.

"No, but I'm sure you will tell me."

"You can never leave the past."

"And you, dear brother, can never look at it."

Then in December at my yearly gynecological checkup, the tests showed precancerous cells. I wasn't given time to think twice. I visited Chuck on the 17th and on the 20th underwent surgery—a full hysterectomy, luckily the laparoscopic kind. I did manage to get to Marcia's for Christmas. For the first and only time I can remember, there's not one entry in the calendar on my birthday. On the 4th of January 2000, Chuck made the decision to die. He called Marcia first just as she was moving out of her house. Whether I was next on the list or after his former mistress, made no difference. I went back up to White Plains to be with him, at ten at night he told me to go home. I had been resting on a chaise they had brought into his room. His intense anger which had raged for months now abated. I stood on the platform of the train station wondering if he would last the night. At 9 o'clock the next morning, as I came onto his floor, the nurse informed me he was gone.

He looked so peaceful. I kissed him goodbye. His wife appeared, having flown up the night before. Upon seeing him she became hysterical. I had no empathy or sympathy. Their marriage—the fault of both—had been what I called a dance of death. Marcia came and took care of her. I went home. That afternoon Chuck's wife called. "I don't want to remember him that way. I need you to take a picture of him after they fix him up."

Like an idiot, I promised. I called Campbell's—the funeral parlor. "Can I see him? I need to take a picture."

"Sure, we get these requests all the time. Sometimes there's even a party. He'll be ready tomorrow morning. Come when you like."

The man ushered me into an enormous huge empty room. All the way at the far end lay my brother on what appeared to be a table, pale as a ghost, no pun intended. I really thought he'd looked better before they'd embalmed him. I headed towards him and then from some place deep inside, and as a total surprise to me, I let out the loudest, "What the fuck have you left me with!" The Campbell's man ran out of the room. Who could blame him? I had appeared so rational a few moments before. I snapped a few shots and left. His wife never asked for the pictures and I hid them behind some books. Contrary to my normal "tear and toss" impulses, they remained in my possession for way too long. The funeral, as one friend put it, was the worst one she'd ever attended. If there was a kind word, it was hard to find. Shiva, or whatever you would call the gathering, took place at my loft. I have no idea where my brother's ashes are. I presume with his wife. The last place he wanted to be.

I think what I found the strangest part of the next few years was how little I missed Susanne. She had always said that at a certain point the good-enough-mother gets internalized and then is no longer needed. It would have been wonderful to have discovered I actually had developed an inner core with her still alive, but it was not to be.

For a period of time I became friends with the two couples who had been Susanne's mainstays—my fantasy of being accepted into her world of intelligentsia spoiled by the reality. Yes, one couple were academics, and all four individuals were lovely people, but they had their own lives, own friends, own families. As the friendships were built on our attachment to Susanne, the cord that held us frayed over time until there was no more than perhaps a phone call here, a card there, and then nothing.

Within weeks of Chuck's funeral and my surgery, I was back on the road, holding workshops, some for small groups, others for audiences of eighty five and more. The client list continued to expand and between the cats and work, a few dinners here or there, there's little of note to report.

A word should be said about 9/11. That morning, unlike every other morning of my life unless I was ill, I woke unable to down my usual glass of juice, coffee, and toast. I had no appetite, no desire for coffee—even though I'm an admitted addict. As it was a primary Election Day, I bathed, dressed and prepared to go vote. The television on, I listened to Matt Lauer and Katie Couric's banter, waiting for hunger to set in. When it didn't, at about 8:45 I left the loft and went downstairs to see a group of people on the corner all transfixed on something downtown. "What happened?" I asked as I got to them.

"A plane went into one of the Towers. It was flying so low. We could see it pass by right here."

From where we stood, a few miles away, smoke could be seen coming out the side of the building. The picture that immediately came to mind was that of a floor in the Empire State Building after a small plane crashed there in 1948. Even though one of the onlookers had said it looked like a freight plane, I wasn't able to put it together. It didn't make sense to me to stand and watch, so I went up the block, voted, came back, and seeing the crowd still there, figured I would learn more by going home and watching TV. Once there I remained glued only getting up to call friends and clients on their cells who I knew worked in and around those buildings to see if they needed a place to stay until they found a way home. The odors began to seep through my windows, but I will not say much more on the subject, because I personally didn't know anyone who died (though I had clients who did nothing but attend funerals for the next weeks.) Because of the asthma, I couldn't go down to Ground Zero and volunteer as a friend did; I did however go to one of my doctors' offices the next day and play receptionist as his couldn't get into the city. The emptiness of the streets was unsettling; the pictures going up of lost ones were as well. But it wasn't until a few weeks later, when I was conducting a workshop in Boston, did I realize I had not escaped totally unscathed. I stood at the head of the conference table, my back to the door. There were windows opposite me which looked out across to Logan Airport. Every plane that took off went straight up, then made a turn and appeared to be coming directly at us. I began to shake uncontrollably and we closed the blinds.

My twice a week walks to and from Susanne were as if they had never occurred. Whereas for years, walking near where Mother had lived caused tears to flow and me to flee, I could wander Susanne's neighborhood and not feel a thing. Maybe her, "We mourn what could have been, not what was," explains the difference. She had given me all I needed. I had a career, friends, and was able to write without it engulfing me.

The Last of the Lovers

A week before I was to turn 64, I stepped into my elevator and there he was: tall, well-built—sheepskin jacket with jeans—dark hair, dark eyes with a flicker, let me repeat, dark eyes with a flicker— that magnetic tease.

"Haven't seen you here before. Do you work here?" I asked referring to the floor where he had gotten on.

"Yes, started a while ago."

The accent familiar, I asked in my limited German, "Wovon?" From where?

Of course I knew from red flags, but at that stage in my life, what harm could there be? And I'd been celibate for so damn long. Of course, my nose ferreted out he was passive aggressive on scent, but as Dr. B would have said, there was no stopping me. I rode the elevator, more than necessary, to see if we'd run into each other again. We did and he asked for my card. Or maybe I gave it to him. Who remembers? He said he would call. It took one more not so accidental meeting for him to say he was going for a walk and would I like to join. Okay, I made conversation until he had no choice but to ask. We headed up to Central Park. He already had dinner plans and said he could come by after. Now any self-respecting woman would have at least said, no, perhaps another night. But let's face it, I wanted to get laid. So I waited and waited well past the hour he said he'd arrive and when he did, I let him in. He admitted to having purposely put me through the wait just to see if I was the demanding type. And oh! Did I mention? He was 39, but then, in my mind I was still 46.

He said he'd been married to a woman my age, making it obvious to me that I'd be his transition into a more appropriate relationship. I even bet I looked like her. It took him months to admit this was true. We were totally mismatched except in bed. We called it quits, three months later—truth: he did. Now we both knew from day one this was not going to last, but I wasn't ready to let him go even though, except for bed, I was totally bored. Still, I wept for a year. I didn't miss him specifically—we had been all about sex and little else—though he could cook. No, I cried because I knew in my heart he would be the last of the wine. My men had all been affairs, never long involved relationships. Any man of a certain age would most likely be a widower wanting a widow. Someone who shared their particular life style. And my life style was to be alone. Eventually my 39 year old left the city, married, moved to London and the elevator became neutral territory once again.

Warner Books decided not to have another printing of my book, so I took back the rights and set about self-publishing it. An incredible amount had to be rewritten and updated. Between 1997 and 2003 technology had changed the way we lived. It was a whole new world. Slides once replaced by overheads were now replaced by Power Point and other computer programs. What had not changed was the psychology behind how we present ourselves to an audience—and those chapters remained the same. Susanne had taught me well. I published it in 2003 with a simple red, white, and black cover and my name spelled correctly. I kept the old title—it made no sense to change it.

In September of '03, I attended a party my cousin Charles threw for all the cousins. He had just finished building his house and the concrete steps leading from it to the street were not yet lit. As we were leaving, around eleven at night, the lift of my shoe got caught and I fell, slamming my head onto the stone. There were no railings and for whatever reason, I didn't try to break my fall with my hands. My glasses shattered but thankfully I only sustained a hairline fracture around the eye socket. I looked like hell for over a week, but it could have been much worse.

Simultaneous to the fall, I started having extreme night sweats—extreme being the operative word. My mattress would be soaked through when I woke. And I felt lousy, found eating almost impossible—even walking across the room became quite difficult. In between tests to find out what was wrong, I saw clients, at home, often wrapped in a blanket on the sofa. Finally, towards the end of November, a new doctor put it all together. I had something called Temporal Arteritis, an inflammation of the temporal artery which left untreated can cause blindness, even death. I was given massive doses of steroids reduced over time until the condition disappeared. By December, still on steroids, I was well enough to hold a workshop at a client's offices; she was kind enough to let me conduct it sitting down.

By now I was sixty-six and on Medicare. My business was thriving. My life appeared quite good except for worry about my cats who weren't faring particularly well. (I am well aware that one should use "that" for cats vs. "who", but they were my children and every bit a person as anyone I knew.) For a very brief period I took up ballroom dancing which sent me into a crazed high—one friend said it was like I was in heat. Possibly. My German lover's departure left me feeling sexless. Doing the rumba brought back all the feelings I'd had dancing with my brother years before—even with a gay teacher, the rumba can be quite sensual. But it was not to last. I stood up one day and the knee gave way. I will not put the reader through the knee saga only to say that it's been replaced, although not soon enough.

By 2006 I began seriously to contemplate leaving the loft. Thoughts that it was not a place in which to grow old began creeping up in my early 60's. Not on a daily or even weekly basis, but here and there like when I slipped off the steps leading from the kitchen, fell flat on the floor and realized there was no way someone could come to my aid if needed, as you had to have a key for the downstairs doors, the elevators to one's particular floor, as well as the front door. Or when I broke my leg and had to use a wheelchair which didn't fit through either of my bathroom doors. Maybe if I'd been a healthier specimen it wouldn't have dawned so early that a building without a doorman—or at least a live-in Super—might not be the best place to age alone, but as stated, I wasn't always in the best of shape. (Illness is lousy at any point, but one's mortality is brought home when it coincides with the aging process.) Still, as I saw it, there was plenty of time to consider moving out—perhaps in my mid to late 80's, if then. Now I was getting close to 70 and the 80's didn't seemed that far away. I began hinting to friends I was considering selling the loft. "Get off it! The only way you're leaving, is feet first," the universal reply. Their reaction understandable. At that point, I'd lived and worked in the space for over thirty years. To those who knew me, the loft and I were synonymous. Thankfully, the real estate agent I contacted was extraordinarily honest. "Don't sell now, she said. "Eaterly is opening around the corner from you as well as Trader Joe's. Besides, you're not ready." And she was right. I wasn't.

The Loft at 20th Street

My creative side had lain dormant for some time. Sitting at my computer one day, simultaneously speaking on the phone to a friend, I bemoaned that my life felt empty. Besides work what was there? I had way too much time to fill. She went through the litany of things I could do: take a class, plan a trip, find a hobby, go back to drawing, and to each I responded with: Been there; done that. Finally, in total exasperation, she asked, "What haven't you done?"

To which I replied, "Well, I haven't written a play."

"Then type in New York City Playwrights and see what comes up."

And voila! Something did. Started by a playwright it was a place where one could get scenes read by actors who showed up to do cold readings. I started to write again. That led to a workshop held by Gretchen Cryer at The Cherry Lane Theater and that led to my working with her privately for two years on a play about Susanne. (I'm considering a total rewrite.) This was 2010.

In July, I dropped Benji off at the vet for one last test, went to work with Gretchen, then returned to the vet for what I knew the verdict would be. It was time to put the last of my long line of cats down. (Kirle had died the year before.) That night two friends took me out. While they drank and ate, I downed five Margaritas, not one of which I felt. The loss of Benji whom I had adored, and who had been sick for a year—one in which I often hoped he would pass—was unbearable. He had slept alongside my body, sat next to me at the counter when I ate, and carried on conversations, startling guests. Here too, like my last lover, it was the knowledge that a part of my life was over. There would never be another animal I could watch move elegantly across my room, fall down in front of me for my entertainment, slowly push cans of food off the kitchen counter to get my attention. No, I could not imagine moving into my 80's worried about which of us would go first. Nor could I consider dealing with another loss.

Benji

The next year, after two readings of the play for friends, I turned to putting a number of my stories into book form. I hired an editor who taught me more about writing than the few classes I had taken over the years. I self-published the book in 2012. (For those who read the first nine stories, you can now decipher fact from fiction.) The good news about both the play and the book is that nowhere did either take over my life. I did not fly off into fantasy that I was now a playwright or a writer. Yes, I shopped the play around and tried to find an agent for the book before self-publishing, but when I had no success there, it wasn't a problem.

On my 75th birthday I made the decision to sell the loft. I was more than ready. The dampness in the loft in both the fall and spring had become more and more difficult for me to deal with—arthritis having set in. I longed for more creature comforts. Something cozier, more homey in feel. As for the workshops, they had become too repetitive. There were few if any surprises. If I had to say the same words one more time, I thought I'd scream. And I believed, rightly so, that if I was going to make the move, I had to do so when I physically could, not when I needed to. So in January 2013, I called my real estate gal. "It's time!" I said and began preparing to leave a home which had defined me; move out of a neighborhood and a world I'd called home for most of my adult life, disposing of most of my belongings with a vengeance. It was as if someone had said the only way you can start over is by arriving at your next destination empty handed.

I Was There All Along

June 2016

I sit at my desk. The sun pours in. The view wonderful. To my left, rows of beautifully kept town houses and just behind them, the back of a church—the rear wall filled with stained glass oriel windows cut into the bricks. Opposite, set back from the street—an apartment house with terraces rarely if ever used. To the right: a block lined with trees. Looking down from my seventh floor perch, I see a hodgepodge of people: some well-dressed, some in gym clothes, some in business attire, others of the workmen variety. There are dog walkers, pregnant women, baby carriage pushers all walking to different rhythms. When I first moved here all I noticed were the old people with walkers, wheelchairs, and aides—portents of things to come. Now with my new knee allowing me to function normally the aged blend into the landscape.

Ironically, I am seven blocks from where my mother lived; over forty from the loft. At my interview with the Co-op Board of this building, the first question asked was "Why uptown?" I sat there stupefied. Only minutes before, as I'd waited to be called in, I'd been on the phone with Marcia asking the very same question. "What the hell am I doing? I'm a downtown gal, for God's sake!" It was only when the head of the Board said, "You're a communications coach and you can't answer a question?" that I found my voice. "The apartment makes sense. It's age appropriate." And it is. There are people in the building who can help me when needed—and I have heat. Recently I referred to the apartment as the loft—perhaps I meant I was home.

I do sometimes wonder if I had switched therapists—one that might have focused on the man issue—would my life have changed, but I doubt it would have made much difference. Did I tell you about the time a couple called to say they'd found me the perfect man? A day later my back went out. X-rays showed a twisted spine. Theories were advanced: I had thrown it out lifting a sculpture; a disc had dislodged, and so on. Still an evening was planned—I didn't cancel even though I was crippled in pain—the couple entered, followed by "the" man. He was arrogant, bombastic and definitely not the one. My back went into place within seconds. So clearly I'm more comfortable alone even though, from habit, I automatically check out the ring finger of every attractive man who gets into the elevator.

Of course, I still wrestle with whether or not to spend a dime. The night "L" had taken Dorothy and me to the Russian Tea Room I got into an intense argument with the waiter over which Shashlik to order. There were two on the menu, one, I'm serious, 25 cents more than the other. The waiter, one of the old timers, a waiter-for-life not an actor auditioning for a role, told me to take the more expensive one. I couldn't. Dorothy had told me "L" was in financial difficulties—what with all his exes rightly demanding alimony. The argument got extremely heated until the waiter left in a fury. All right, 25 cents in 1967 would be approximately $1.75 today (I checked), but if "L" could afford the Russian Tea Room, he certainly could have afforded the $1.75. Yet this afternoon I permitted myself to save a trip to the post office and ordered stamps on line for an additional $1.30—an enormous improvement.

And I'm constantly amazed by how many people seek my counsel even as I let "Speak UP!" die of attrition. For the most part I'm turning down jobs that come in, though there's one that I promised to take. How could I not? It came from a colleague of my first client Lisa, the anesthesiologist, requesting my services to work with his doctors. It's too neat a bow to tie not to accept. And as for my days, well I spend them writing. Not that I'd ever refer to myself as a writer. I am a woman who writes, just as I once was one who sculpted. It's more than okay. It's who I am.

Nowadays

Made in the USA
Middletown, DE
23 April 2017